THE PRETZEL MAN

A True Story of Phobias and Back Problems

By

James C. Schaefer

ISBN: 1-4033-6508-3 (e-book)
ISBN: 1-4033-6509-1 (Paperback)
ISBN: 1-4033-6510-5 (Hardcover)

Library of Congress Control Number: 2002093974

This book is printed on acid free paper.

Printed in the United States of America
Bloomington, IN

1stBooks - rev. 11/09/02

DISCLAIMER

This book is a true story of the author's experiences with back problems, phobias, Thought Field Therapy (TFT), etc. He makes various suggestions based on his experiences.

The author of The Pretzel Man has no medical background and is not affiliated with any TFT practitioners.

Before attempting any techniques, therapies, or strategies described in this book, the author suggests you first discuss them with a psychologist, medical doctor or religious counsel.

The author assumes no responsibility, whatsoever, for the effectiveness of techniques, therapies and strategies suggested in this book.

INTRODUCTION

Many books have been written by psychologists regarding the treatment of individuals who were diagnosed as having a neurosis. In general, I find that those books are filled with anecdotes of individuals suffering from depression and other psychological problems, of treatments lasting a number of months, and of clients that recover and resume their normal lives. Infrequently is there a case where the problem is unresolved.

Very few, if any, books have been written by clients who were treated for a neurosis on strictly an outpatient basis. If they had written their stories, I think those books would be filled with reports of years spent in treatment. Many would report their neurosis was never resolved. (There have, of course, been a number of books written by individuals whose cases required them to be institutionalized in mental hospitals.)

This book is unique. It is a true story of psychological problems and outpatient treatments, but written from a client–not psychologist–viewpoint.

I led a normal life until age 36–no childhood problems, no divorced parents, no health problems. I breezed through grade school, high school and college. I had a dream job. I spent my free time playing sports.

Then my life collapsed. Suddenly I had horrendous back problems. Later my daily life was dominated by phobias. Initially, I had a fear of utility companies. Then I developed a fear of the state of Wisconsin. That fear grew until I had a phobia that encompassed almost all of the states in the Midwest.

Ultimately, I was able to resolve my psychological problems. However, it only occurred after 20-plus years of effort, a lucky referral to a Thought Field Therapy (TFT) practitioner, and my own eureka experience.

This book is divided into two parts. The first part is a narrative in which I describe–in chronological sequence–the problems I encountered, my various attempts at solving the problems, and then finally successful resolution.

The second part is a discussion of how individuals with psychological problems can use my experiences to resolve their problems–the primary purpose of this book. My recommendations are considerably different from what you'll find in a typical psychology book, but based on personal experience.

Anyone contemplating psychotherapy will find this book useful. If you choose Thought Field Therapy (TFT), you'll have a good idea of what to expect.

I kept a diary through the years. This book is based on my diary and, of course, my memories of the events. When the entries in my diary were not sufficiently explicit, I relied on my memory to describe the events as best I could.

Except where I give the full name, all names of persons are fictitious.

In the beginning of my 20-plus-years saga, I suffered from severe back problems. These were the manifestations: My hips were pulled four inches to the right; my neck was tilted to the right; my head and shoulders leaned forward; my right leg and foot were twisted outward. I was a contorted mess. Hence: The Pretzel Man.

TABLE OF CONTENTS

PART 1 1

Chapter 01 THE INITIAL PROBLEM.................................. 3

Chapter 02 THE CHIROPRACTOR..................................... 10

Chapter 03 CONTINUING PROBLEMS................................ 15

Chapter 04 THE SURPRISE 19

Chapter 05 MY RESIGNATION 22

Chapter 06 A NEW JOB 26

Chapter 07 A JOB AT MANPOWER, INC. 28

Chapter 08 CALIFORNIA DREAMING 30

Chapter 09 MORE JOB CHANGES.................................. 32

Chapter 10 THE CALIFORNIA CURE 37

Chapter 11 A COUNTY JOB 39

Chapter 12 CALIFORNIA – THE FIRST 6 MONTHS...... 41

Chapter 13 MORE SURPRISES 43

Chapter 14 POSSIBLE RETURN TO WISCONSIN
ELECTRIC 46

Chapter 15 A BANK JOB 47

Chapter 16 THE YEARS 1983 AND 1984 50

Chapter 17 SELLING MY CAR...................................... 53

Chapter 18 BUYING GOLD RIMMED GLASSES 54

Chapter 19 GOALS ACCOMPLISHED 56

Chapter 20 THE 1985 FLIGHT...................................... 58

Chapter 21 ONGOING FEARS 61

Chapter 22 BUYING A CAR.. 64

Chapter 23 PSYCHOTHERAPY 66

Chapter 24 MORE HYPNOSIS 69

Chapter 25 THE ACTIVATOR 72

Chapter 26 BUYING A HOME 74

Chapter 27 THE 2:00 A.M. WAKE-UP 80

Chapter 28 BEING SQUEEZED 84

Chapter 29 MY TEETH 88

Chapter 30 COPING TECHNIQUES 91

Chapter 31 THOUGHT FIELD THERAPY (TFT) 94

Chapter 32 TFT – TOXINS 99

Chapter 33 TFT – DR. ROGER J. CALLAHAN 102

Chapter 34 TFT – FAILED ATTEMPTS 105

Chapter 35 TFT – ONE YEAR REVIEW 107

Chapter 36 THE BREAKTHROUGH 110

Chapter 37 BUYING ANOTHER CAR 113

Chapter 38 CASHING MY CHECKS 115

Chapter 39 IMPROVEMENTS IN THE NEXT YEAR 117

Chapter 40 ANOTHER JOB RESIGNATION 121

Chapter 41 RETIREMENT – THE FIRST 6 WEEKS 123

Chapter 42 8-WEEK VACATION IN WISCONSIN 125

Chapter 43 ANOTHER BREAKTHROUGH SESSION ... 127

Chapter 44 A HAPPY ENDING 129

PART 2 133

Chapter 45 INTRODUCTION – PART 2 135

Chapter 46 A CHANGE IN ENVIRONMENT 136

Chapter 47 WORDS AND PICTURES AND YOUR

NEUROSIS 141

Chapter 48 PSYCHOTHERAPY – SUCCESS AND
FAILURE RATES 145

Chapter 49 WHICH PSYCHOTHERAPY WORKS BEST 149

Chapter 50 WHAT TO DO 151

Chapter 51 TFT – THE THERAPY I RECOMMEND 156

Chapter 52 TFT – VOICE TECHNOLOGY VERSUS
DIAGNOSTIC THERAPIST 157

Chapter 53 CHIROPRACTIC TREATMENTS 160

Chapter 54 NORGESIC PILLS 162

Chapter 55 REPORT THE RECOVERY PERCENTAGE 163

Chapter 56 SUMMARY 170

HOW TO CONTACT THE AUTHOR 172

APPENDIX "A" – CHIROPRACTOR CHART 173

PART 1

A TRUE STORY IN CHRONOLOGICAL SEQUENCE

James C. Schaefer

Chapter 01 THE INITIAL PROBLEM

In the beginning I didn't have a phobia. Initially I had a back problem. Following is an account of how–at age 36 –my back problem started.

The meeting was held on March 19, 1975. The entire committee was present. The chairman was a systems analyst from the Computer Department. There were four members: three systems analysts, including me, from various departments and one labor relations technician from the Personnel Department. We were employees of the Wisconsin Electric Power Co., located in Milwaukee, Wisconsin.

Our committee was established in June 1971. We were to develop a new computerized payroll-personnel system. We had been struggling for four years to develop the new system–at least I thought we had been struggling. It was obvious we were far from completing our project.

By now, we had well-established patterns for holding meetings and performing development work. Basically, the chairman–his name was Arthur–did most of the talking and made the final decisions based on his predetermined concepts. He had one other important trait: He never allowed an idea to be developed in full detail. I had seethed under those practices. I thought we weren't developing anything that was usable.

The March 19 meeting ran true to form. The chairman explained that the computerized system would need to provide for a new type of standby pay. He asked that we determine what changes would be required to the new payroll-personnel system. He then said that we would meet in two days to finalize the required changes.

I didn't say anything at the meeting. But I immediately recognized that this was another assignment to be completed using the "don't develop in detail" concept. We didn't have a full description of the new standby pay, wouldn't be able to determine how to process it through the new system, and certainly wouldn't be ready to finalize in two days. It would be another partially-developed specification, and our system specifications binders were loaded with partially-developed specs.

As I walked back to my desk from the meeting, I said to myself, "That's it. I'm getting off this committee."

Getting removed from the committee wouldn't be easy. I knew I'd need a good scheme to do it.

I started working for Wisconsin Electric as a systems analyst trainee in June 1961, my first job after graduating from college with a business administration major. I spent my first four years as an analyst in electric service billing, spent the next four years as a computer programmer, and then spent the following six years as a systems analyst responsible for payroll programs and procedures. In short, I was well qualified to be on the committee.

I had tried to be reassigned from the committee a year earlier, but it had been a lukewarm effort. My supervisor, Bradford, had declined to reassign me.

I decided to use "health problems" as a way to get off the committee. I had missed only a few days due to illness during my 14 years at the Company, and I figured some sick time would get the attention of my supervisor. On the Thursday and Friday following the March 19 meeting, I called in sick.

I reported to work on the following Monday and immediately asked my supervisor for a meeting with him. We met at 10:00 a.m. I told him that I had been absent on Thursday and Friday due to "nervousness." I said that I had been on the computerization committee for four years, that I thought the project was going nowhere, and that the project was making me so anxious my overall health was being affected. I then asked to be removed from the committee.

I knew that any decision my supervisor made would have to be approved by Michael, our manager. What I said next surprised even me, because I hadn't rehearsed it. I said, "You think that Michael and you can decide which analysts will work on this project. That's not true in this case. If I don't get off this project, I'm not going to be here. I'm going to be out sick."

The following week, my supervisor informed me that I was off the computerization committee. My strategy had worked.

4

I think there were two factors that helped get me off the committee. I had reported to my supervisor for ten years, and we had an excellent working relationship. I think he wanted me healthy and working for him. Also, I had previously written two memos to Michael, our manager, that criticized the work of our computerization committee. When a committee member isn't in sync with the committee, it's often advisable to remove the member.

The computerization committee had occupied 40% of my time, and ongoing payroll work had taken up the rest of my time. To give me a full work load, I was given some assignments in electric service billing.

There was one negative item that resulted from my removal from the committee. Michael stopped talking to me.

I was so pleased about getting off the committee that I thought I should take a vacation to celebrate. I checked with my best buddy, and it turned out he and his wife were planning to take a trip to California in April. He invited me to join them.

We planned a 7-day vacation and left for San Francisco on Sunday, April 20. We spent 5 days in San Francisco, and we did the usual tourist activities—i.e., bus tour of the city, visit to Fisherman's Wharf, evening meals at nice restaurants, etc.

On my second day in San Francisco, I started limping a little and had pain in my right leg. I assumed it would clear up in a day or two. Little did I realize that this was the start of a severe back problem.

In planning the trip, I had arranged to spend five days in San Francisco and two days in Reno, Nevada. (I had never been to Reno.) On April 25, I flew to Reno. My two days in Reno were not good. By now, I had a severe limp and fairly significant pain in my right leg. I spent some time at the gambling casinos, but mainly I was interested in getting home and seeing a doctor.

On the Monday following my return from Reno, I phoned my osteopath for an appointment. He had solved two earlier medical problems for me, and I had full confidence he would resolve my leg problem.

Following is a description of the two earlier times that I saw my osteopath. In 1971, I threw out my back when I bent over to pick up a baseball bat. I had never before had a back problem. Also, I didn't have a regular doctor. So I just looked in the yellow pages and picked a doctor. Luckily I picked an osteopath. He treated me with diathermy, back manipulation, and prescribed a muscle relaxant. I recovered in a few days. I had a similar experience a couple years later, and my osteopath again quickly resolved it.

I saw my osteopath on Monday afternoon. He examined me and explained that my leg pain was "referred pain." (Referred pain is pain that is felt in a particular area of the body, but originates somewhere else in the body.) He said that my back was causing the pain, and that I had sciatica. He treated me in the same manner as in my prior visits.

This time the treatment didn't work as well. There was some improvement, but my limp and some pain remained.

I saw my osteopath once a week. By the end of May–treatment for about a month–I was doing fairly well. Recovery looked in sight.

Then on Sunday, June 8, 1975, my health problem took a dramatic turn for the worse. I woke up feeling sick and immediately sensed that my back was not right. I looked in a mirror and saw that my hips were shifted four inches to the right. My head was tilted significantly to the right, to maintain a balanced body. My head and shoulders leaned forward. After a closer look, I noted that my right leg and foot were twisted outward. In general, I had lots of muscles that felt tense and sore.

Prior to this Sunday, my back and hips had been in their normal, aligned positions.

The pain in my leg had increased significantly. The leg pain was in the area of the calf muscle, about four inches above the ankle. I did not have any pain in my lower back.

Although I was twisted out of shape, I was able to report to work the next day. I worked in the Methods Division, and the practice was to prepare a time sheet each morning for the preceding day. Each analyst would turn in his or her time sheet to the supervisor.

I walked into the supervisor's office with my time sheet. He looked up at me and saw my unusual posture. "What happened to you?" he asked.

"Nothing, it just came on," I replied.

I saw my osteopath twice that week. The first treatment had no significant effect. After my second treatment, he said, "I think we should leave your back alone for awhile. Let's schedule your next

6

appointment for a month from now." I didn't think much of that idea. But I agreed.

I was taking a muscle relaxant called Norgesic. I required eight tablets a day, two tablets at a time. The tablets were very effective and would take away the pain completely. During the day, I would take the tablets every 6 to 8 hours. However when I slept, the effect would only last 4 to 5 hours. If I went to bed at 11:00 p.m., the pain in my leg would be severe enough to wake me at 3:30 a.m. My normal routine was to get up between 3:00 a.m. and 4:00 a.m. to take two Norgesic tablets.

The headquarters of Wisconsin Electric Power Co. was located in downtown Milwaukee. I lived in an apartment about a mile from headquarters, and I walked to and from work each day. Because of my back condition, I could no longer walk a mile. I started driving my car to work.

Although my condition fluctuated slightly from day to day, my basic back problem remained the same. I looked forward to my next appointment with the osteopath.

After a month had passed, I went back to see my osteopath. He examined me and suggested I see him in three months. He did not treat me–i.e., no back manipulation, etc. I was upset. I knew his "see me in three months" meant he was dropping my case.

Because I hadn't had many medical problems, I wasn't too familiar with operations in the medical profession. I had assumed that if my osteopath couldn't help me, he would refer me to some medical specialist.

My best buddy had married a Filipino doctor. I phoned her to find out what I should do next. She said I needed to see an orthopedic surgeon. But I should first see a general practitioner. The general practitioner would refer me to the orthopedic surgeon.

Within a week, I was in to see a general practitioner, Dr. Ray. Sometimes when you see a doctor, you feel like you're presenting yourself when your condition isn't at its worst point. The day I saw Dr. Ray I was at my worst. I looked bad and I felt lousy. He examined me and then handed me off to a technician to get some X-rays taken.

The X-ray technician had me step up on a stand that was about six inches high. I almost couldn't get on the stand; then I came close to falling off of it. And I was only 37 years old. (I had turned 37 on June 8, 1975.)

After the X-rays were taken, I saw Dr. Ray again. He didn't prescribe any treatment, except for suggesting that I do exercises. He gave me a one-page sheet that described the exercises.

I said, "Exercises! Until I got this back problem, I was spending all my free time playing sports. I play tennis, volleyball, softball and touch football. During the summer, I play softball two nights a week and tennis on Saturday and Sunday. In the winter, I play tennis and volleyball indoors."

He said, "The sports you're playing aren't exercising the right back muscles."

"I find that hard to believe," I commented.

I did the exercises he suggested for two, maybe three, days. Even those limited exercises increased the pain in my leg. I decided I wasn't going to do exercises. Besides, I didn't think my problem was caused by a lack of exercise.

A week later I saw the orthopedic surgeon. He examined me and set up an appointment to see a neurologist. He said I should see him again, after I had seen the neurologist.

As I was being processed through these appointments with the general practitioner, orthopedic surgeon, etc., I was quite upbeat. I felt I had gotten into a network of doctors who would solve my problem.

Ten days later, I saw the neurologist. He gave me an extensive EMG (electromyogram) examination, but I wasn't too happy with it. Basically the exam consisted of electrical shocks. Presumably, he was stimulating a nerve in one part of the body and checking to see if the stimulation was transmitted to another part of the body.

I think he had the amperage set too high, because I was getting really shocked. As a patient you're so engrossed in getting through a procedure you usually don't get involved in making suggestions–like turn down the amperage.

That examination took place over 25 years ago, and it still irritates me. I had never been operated on. (Children in my generation normally had their tonsils and adenoids removed. I still had mine.) In the lexicon of doctors, there had been no trauma. In short, that doctor was working with virgin material. In his medical wisdom, he apparently thought zapping me was the way to go.

In late August, I saw the orthopedic surgeon again. He showed me the neurologist's report. It was written in technical language that I didn't understand. However, the gist of it was that I had a pinched nerve (sciatica). That wasn't news to me. The osteopath had provided me with that same information three months earlier.

The orthopedic surgeon asked if I was doing exercises for my back. I said, "No, I'm not going to do exercises. They increase the pain."

He said, "Well, the only other option would be surgery."

"Surgery! I'm not going to have surgery," I said.

In my reply I had simply rejected his suggestion of surgery. Inside I was furious. From his examination and comments, I knew he didn't even know where to cut. A surgery area defined as somewhere in the lower back isn't nearly precise enough. I couldn't get over how stupid his suggestion was. I never saw him again.

I had spent one and a half months seeing the general practitioner, neurologist and orthopedic surgeon. None of them had given me any help. In fact, I thought their advice wasn't even reasonable.

I was able to work each day, and I was enjoying my work assignments. But after that, I was in sad shape. I hadn't played any sports since March 1975–a 5-month layoff. Two blocks was the farthest I could walk. I couldn't lift a bag of groceries. I didn't see any other medical options that I could pursue.

I thought my life was over.

Chapter 02 THE CHIROPRACTOR

On the first Friday in September 1975, a most fortuitous event occurred. I was walking down a hallway at work when it happened. Not walking briskly you understand. I was in my usual bad-back posture, with my hips shifted to the right and my head and shoulders tilted slightly forward and down.

A stranger came up to me and said, "Why in the hell don't you see a chiropractor."

I raised my head and eyes to look at him. "Do you have the name of one?"

"Yeah, Dr. Fox. He's in the phone book."

"I'll call him." I phoned Dr. Fox and set up an appointment.

At 1:30 p.m. that afternoon I was in the office of Dr. Edward V. Fox. (His office was located in Wauwatosa, a suburb of Milwaukee.) He had about ten leg braces hanging on one wall in his waiting room. I assumed they were leg braces that patients of his had once used, but no longer needed.

Dr. Fox greeted me and motioned me into his office. He asked me to undress to the waist. I described the problems I was having. He didn't say much. He examined my back and said, "For first-time patients, I sometimes take X-rays. I don't need any X-rays for your case. I'll adjust your back first." ("Adjust" is the term chiropractors use to describe the manipulation of the back and other parts of the body that they perform.)

He then had me lie on a small (6 feet long, 3 feet wide, and 3 feet high) leather-covered table. He then "adjusted" my back—a couple of times. My back was quite sore. So each adjustment resulted in a few seconds of pain. Overall, not a bad experience. It took maybe 10 minutes.

He then asked me to move to another area in his office. As I stood facing him, he reached out and touched the side of my neck with one finger. He said, "Part of your problem is your neck. You're sore right here." The spot he touched was indeed tender and sore. I was impressed.

None of the doctors I had previously seen had been able to identify any place that was tender to the touch.

He had me lie on a table that was designed for adjusting the neck. He adjusted my neck, using what I call the karate chop method. He put the side of his hand on the side of my neck and applied a quick, sharp pressure. In other words, downward pressure from the side of the hand for a fraction of a second and then release. He did this twice.

After he had completed the adjusting of my neck, I stood up. He again touched the side of my neck with his finger and said, "Now that should feel less tender." It did.

He set up an appointment for the following Monday.

As I drove back to my office, I checked my body. I put my hand on my neck and rubbed it several times. Mentally I checked my back. Everything seemed to be okay. At least he hadn't done any damage. And I felt good.

That night (Friday) I went to bed at 11:00 p.m., a little earlier than usual. I woke to the alarm clock at 8:00 a.m. I shut off the alarm, decided I was still tired and went back to sleep. The next time I woke it was 3:00 p.m. I had slept 16 hours straight.

I was really pleased. I got up and checked my back. I couldn't detect any changes. Regardless, I figured that much sleep couldn't be anything but a good sign.

On the following Monday, I saw Dr. Fox for the second time. He treated me the same as on Friday–i.e., adjusted my back and neck. This time I did just a quick check of my neck and back as I returned to my office. Everything felt okay.

When I awoke the next morning, I felt incredibly tired. I knew it was the same tiredness I had encountered after the first chiropractor visit. I called in sick and went back to bed. When I finally got up in the afternoon, I checked my back. This time there was a sign of improvement. It looked like my hips had shifted in just a bit. Oh, it was nice to see.

For the next three weeks, that pattern repeated itself. I saw Dr. Fox on Mondays and Fridays. On Tuesdays and Saturdays, I was very tired and slept till late morning or early afternoon.

I checked my back many times each day. I would stand in front of a full-length mirror and look to see if my hips had shifted in.

The news was good. My hips were slowly moving back toward their normal position.

I had a long way to go. There was no change in my leg pain, and I was still taking the Norgesic tablets to eliminate the pain. I was still very weak and couldn't lift a bag of groceries.

Starting in October 1975, Dr. Fox had me see him once a week. The treatment was the same each visit. He would adjust my neck and back.

There were some nice improvements in October. I stopped feeling so tired the day after the chiropractic adjustments, and no longer took sick days to sleep. I began to take walks in the evening. I couldn't walk very far, but I was able to walk farther than the two blocks that had previously been my limit.

By early November 1975, my hips were pulled to the right about 1-1/4 inches–a dramatic improvement from the 4-inch misalignment in June 1975.

Dr. Fox suggested I switch from an appointment every week to one every two weeks. That was fine with me. However, we would soon learn that scheduling wouldn't work.

Beginning in late November, I began to experience incidents where my back condition would change significantly–for the worse. What I experienced would normally be called "throwing out your back." However my back was already out.

This is a description of a typical incident: I might wake in the morning feeling somewhat sick. My eyes would be bothering me, in the sense that I wasn't seeing with my normal acuity. I would sense that my back was worse. I would check in the mirror and find that my hips had shifted right an additional one and three-quarter inches–i.e., my hips were misaligned a total of three inches. It was a most discouraging sight.

I would phone Dr. Fox and ask to see him that same day. He always accommodated me. He would perform the normal adjusting. I would feel better almost immediately. Within 24 hours, my hips would shift from the 3-inch misalignment to the 1 1/4-inch misalignment.

Dr. Fox and I then decided that I should only see him when my back went out. The interval between these back incidents was anywhere from 5 days to 2½ weeks. In other words, I saw him about three times a month.

Although these back incidents were obviously steps backward, my overall condition continued to improve. I started a program of walking every night. I started getting the rhythm back in my walk. I told myself I was walking to improve my back condition. Mainly I think I was walking because I was so pleased I could do it.

By the end of November 1975, I was able to reduce my use of Norgesic tablets to four per day, from the eight I had been taking. I needed those tablets more than I thought.

One time I got careless and ran out of Norgesic tablets. I had taken my prescription to the pharmacist, but he said he couldn't fill the prescription until the next morning. I figured I could use aspirin instead.

That night I took two aspirin before going to bed. Then I took more aspirin. But it didn't work. I had so much sciatic pain I couldn't fall asleep. Obviously, the Norgesic tablets had an extra ingredient that I needed.

I slept very little that night, and the next morning I called in sick. I picked up my Norgesic prescription, took two tablets and went to sleep. I thank God—and 3M Pharmaceuticals—for Norgesic tablets.

In early December 1975, I decided I could resume walking to and from work. It was a 1-mile walk, and the first morning I allowed myself an extra 15 minutes. However I didn't need the additional time. I completed the walk in my usual time.

Walking home that evening was a different story. I started out feeling strong. But after three blocks, I was really weak. I sat down and rested. I made it home, but I had to sit down and rest every block. It took an hour to walk the one mile.

I continued walking to and from work. In a week or so, I was able to walk home in the evening without any rest stops. I had reached a milestone in my recovery.

I've played many sports through the years. Tennis is my favorite. During Christmas week, I decided I could resume my sports activities and arranged to play doubles tennis indoors. I had last played tennis in March, a 9-month absence from the courts.

Oh, my return to the tennis courts went well. I ran, hit ground strokes, and served without any significant limitations. I had some aches in my right leg, but it wasn't a serious problem.

I was back!

Due to four months (Sept. – Dec.) of chiropractic treatment, I went from walking that was limited to two blocks to playing all-out tennis.

Although I resumed playing tennis, my back problem was still not completely resolved. I was still taking Norgesic tablets for leg pain. My hips were still shifted an inch to the right. (In December 1975, my hips had improved by 1/4 inch.) I could barely lift a bag of groceries, and I was still throwing my back out about every two weeks. I viewed these continuing problems as relatively minor.

Chapter 03 CONTINUING PROBLEMS

I assumed that with time I would make a full recovery. However I soon learned that was not going to happen. By the end of April 1976, I recognized that my recovery had stalled. My condition was about the same as in December 1975. In fact, I was even worse in one aspect of my condition.

In prior months when I threw out my back, I could recover within 24 hours of being treated by the chiropractor. In early 1976, there were two occasions when I threw out my back, and it took two to four days to recover. And I spent a lot of that time sick in bed.

It didn't take me long to distinguish between a 24-hour back problem and the two-to-four day variety. I knew I had a two-to-four day problem if I got a single, 1-split-second shot of pain in my back—an event I'm sure many of you will recognize.

Once I got that 1-split-second shot of pain, I would have all sorts of movement problems. Shifting from a sitting (or lying) position to a standing position became a slow, painful effort. Many times I could take only baby steps. Sometimes I would crawl to the bathroom. Of course, once I got there I would still have to get to an upright position.

A friend suggested I try body massage to get my recovery back on track. I found a masseur who was dedicated to the profession. I found the massages relaxing, but the effect didn't last very long. By the next morning, the effect was gone. I went for a massage once a week for six weeks. In the sixth week, my back went out right during the massage. I don't know if the masseur caused my back to go out, or whether by coincidence the back went out by itself during the massage. In any event, I abandoned the massage effort.

By August 1976, I was becoming increasingly concerned about my lack of strength. I could just lift a bag of groceries. But I was so concerned about throwing out my back that normally I wouldn't lift the bag of groceries. Instead, I would carry two or three items at a time–definitely a slow way to get groceries from the car to the kitchen.

One day I was discussing my strength problem with the manager of my apartment building, and she suggested I see a physical therapist. I had never been to a physical therapist, and I thought it was a good idea. I checked the yellow pages, and a few days later I was in the office of a physical therapist. The sign on the office door said: "Physical Therapist - Chiropractor." I asked for an explanation. The doctor assured me he was qualified in both professions.

I described my back problems and the treatments I had received. He said he would give me chiropractic adjustments and also provide me with some exercises to do. I told him I had tried to do exercises, but they had increased the pain.

"You were doing standard exercises that orthopedic doctors recommend. I'll give you different exercises. You'll be able to do these," he said. He gave me some papers with diagrams of the exercises. He suggested I do five different exercises with three repetitions of each–twice a day.

The exercises were simple leg and neck movements, and they only took about 5 minutes. Even though only three repetitions were required, at first I could barely do the exercises. There was no increase in pain. So I incorporated the exercises into my daily routines.

After a few weeks, I increased the number of exercises and repetitions. In September 1976, I bought weight lifting equipment. Using two arms, I could lift a maximum of ten pounds without leg pain.

Even though I did my exercises religiously, the benefits were minimal. I thought my overall strength improved maybe 2%. I tried to go from lifting 10 pounds to 12½ pounds, but couldn't do it.

In the last six months of 1976, I began to have sleeping problems. At first I found I would wake up an hour or so before the alarm time. It occurred sporadically. Later in the year I started waking up in the middle of the night, and staying awake for an hour or more. This too was sporadic.

In September 1976, I started practicing meditation to help my sleeping problem. The meditation consisted of sitting comfortably in a sofa, closing my eyes, and repeating over and over a single word to myself. I performed my 20-minute meditations religiously. But it didn't have any effect, even after several months of adherence to the twice-a-day meditations.

By December 1976, I definitely had a sleeping problem. I was waking early, or in the middle of the night, on a regular basis. And I was waking up in the morning feeling like I had slept poorly.

Generally when faced with a health problem, I didn't have the experience to help me solve it. The sleeping problem was different. I knew what to do. I'll explain.

A couple of years earlier, in 1974, there was a month or two when I experienced slight aches in my chest. I saw my osteopath. He prescribed Valium and directed me to take four (5 mg) pills a day. I soon learned that dosage was way too high.

The immediate result was I started sleeping a lot (10 to 12 hours a day), versus my normal 8 hours. Furthermore, the Valium was slowing down my reflexes. I was playing tennis on the seventh day under this Valium regimen, and I was playing at an atrocious level. My reactions to the ball were much too slow. The solution was obvious: stop taking the Valium. And I did.

So, in 1976, when I started having sleeping problems, I remembered the little pill that made me sleep so much. When I would have an insomnia problem, I would take one 5-mg pill–sometimes one half of a pill. Generally I would then fall asleep quite quickly.

By mid-December 1976, I was using Valium for sleeping purposes about twice a week.

I know there are other solutions for sleeping problems–e.g., sleeping pills. However I consider Valium as "without equal." It puts me to sleep and doesn't have any side effects. (I use the word Valium in this book. Actually I used diazepam, the generic equivalent to Valium.)

My problems continued. I began experiencing pain in the tip of my penis. I saw a urologist about that. He had this medical device that I'll describe as a wire with a cotton swab on the end. It was obvious he was going to insert that into my urethra. "Christ! Do we really have to do this?" I thought.

He did insert the device to the base of my penis. It wasn't something I want to do again, but it wasn't a painful procedure.

I saw the urologist a second time. Of all the doctors I've seen over the years, he's the only one who ever cursed. "God damn it," he said, "I can't find a thing wrong with you."

James C. Schaefer

A few weeks later, I developed yet another medical problem. I became slightly incontinent. When I would make a sharp move, urine would dribble into my briefs. At the end of the day, my briefs would have a urine spot that ranged in size from a dime to a quarter.

There was one bright spot. The sciatic pain in my leg had decreased considerably. Basically I had discontinued my use of Norgesic tablets.

By May 1977, I was feeling overwhelmed. I was throwing out my back—and seeing a chiropractor—about three times a month, missing work due to illness a couple days a month, had a slight pain in the tip of my penis, had a slight incontinence problem, had frequent sleeping problems and was simply too tense. The sleeping problem was really bothering me.

To put this into perspective, I felt I was in poor shape, but better than 2 years earlier when I could only walk two blocks and couldn't play tennis. But clearly I needed further improvements in my health.

Chapter 04 THE SURPRISE

I was eligible for three weeks of vacation each year, and in May 1977, I decided to take a 3-week vacation. I wanted to see if I could use the vacation time to bring my tension and sleeping problems to a more reasonable level.

I planned to stay home all three weeks, with tennis as my main activity. As part of the plan, I scheduled two chiropractor visits. I wanted him to monitor the condition of my back. My vacation started on May 21. The first week of vacation didn't produce any changes–i.e., my Valium use and sleeping problems were the same as when I was working.

The second week my sleeping improved slightly, and I didn't use any Valium. I saw my chiropractor, and he said my back was doing fine. No chiropractic adjustments were needed.

The third week was about the same as the second week. I was doing pretty well on the Valium and sleeping issues. I saw my chiropractor again, and he gave me what he called "two minor chiropractic adjustments."

As my vacation ended, I assessed the three weeks. I had played a lot of tennis. I had increased my exercise program to one hour a day, but I still couldn't lift more than 12½ pounds. My sleeping and tension problems had improved slightly. I was pleased that I had gone three weeks without my back going out.

On Monday, June 13, I returned to work. It was a low-activity day. Mainly I reviewed my in-box papers. Then at 4:00 p.m. my back went out! What a surprise!

"My God," I thought, "This job is causing my back problem."

I had always been very satisfied with my job. The Company and I were a perfect fit. Lo and behold! Something at the Company was causing my back problem.

The fact that my back kicked out the first day I returned to work was not a definitive sign, but it certainly was a red flag. I was

19

pleased that it had occurred. I saw that I now had a chance to resolve my 2-year-old back problem.

I had planned to spend my entire work life at the Company. But if I had to resign to get rid of my back problem, I intended to do it.

My back had really kicked out on me. Also, a tic had developed in one of my neck muscles. I called in sick the next day, Tuesday.

At 11:00 a.m. on Tuesday, I was in my chiropractor's office. I told him I intended to resign from my job. "No, no," he said, "You like your job. Stay with it."

"I'll give myself one week to think about it," I said.

I worked on Wednesday and Thursday of that week. On Thursday night, my back went out again. So I was "off work sick" on Friday.

With the eye-opening experience of my back going out twice in my first week back at work, I tried to determine what work-related items might be the cause. There were three likely reasons:

1. PAYROLL-PERSONNEL COMPUTERIZATION PROJECT
   The project had certainly started my back problem. Maybe I just couldn't get over that disappointment. Maybe I was angry at the project chairman.

2. NEW SUPERVISOR
   I had worked for the same supervisor for 12 years, but he was to retire in a year. The new supervisor had been selected and was being phased in. I was definitely unhappy with the new supervisor. Maybe my assumption that I would be able to work with him wasn't flying.

3. LARGE COMPUTER BILLING SYSTEM
   The electric service billing system at the Wisconsin Electric Power Co. is unbelievably large and complex. I had worked about 10 years in the billing system. However, I had worked as an assistant to a senior analyst or in isolated parts of the system. I was now to be a senior analyst who would have full responsibility for basic billing operations. It was going to be much harder than my

payroll assignment. Maybe the magnitude of the assignment was overwhelming me.

I spent the weekend in turmoil. Yes, my back had gone out twice in that first week. But this might be an initial reaction to returning to work. In the following weeks, I might settle down and the back problem could subside. Also, it's possible that the job at my Company–or a job at any company–raised the stress level just enough to give me a back problem.

One item really made it a tough decision. I knew I couldn't get a job that was better than the one I had. The pay, benefits, work hours, co-workers, cafeteria and job satisfaction were all in the "A" category. It was a dream job. I didn't want to leave the Company.

At this point I was handling my own medical problem. And this was my first case. I knew the chances were good you could solve a medical problem if you quit a job you didn't like. I wasn't so sure that resigning from a job you liked was the way to solve a medical problem.

I considered alternatives: I could delay my decision for a month; I could take a leave of absence; I could transfer to another department.

My gut feeling was that I should resign. And that was my decision as I went to bed Sunday night.

Chapter 05 MY RESIGNATION

By 9:00 a.m. Monday, June 20, 1977, I had submitted my letter of resignation. I stated that I was resigning due to back problems and that my resignation was effective 5:00 p.m. that day.

I soon learned that resigning was not going to be as easy as I thought. By 2:00 p.m. that afternoon, I was in the office of the company doctor. He proposed an alternative. He said he would arrange for me to receive a complete physical examination at University of Wisconsin (UW) Hospital and Clinics in Madison, and that I should then take a 30-day leave of absence. I said, "They're not going to find anything wrong in Madison. I think I should just resign."

He said, "If you don't take the examination in Madison, I'll have you locked up in a mental institution." He was serious. I didn't know if he could do that, but I decided I wasn't in a position to challenge. I agreed to the Madison examination.

I checked into the UW Hospital in Madison on Monday, July 4, 1977. I had never before been hospitalized. Right off, I was introduced to the hospital gown. At first, I couldn't figure out how to put on the contraption. That thing is an abortion. (I never wear a dress–or gown–at home.)

I went through all the predictable routines: patient history, blood tests, X-rays and an orthopedic exam. Also, I took the Minnesota Multiphasic Personality Inventory (MMPI) test and was interviewed by a psychologist. The pace was slow, and I didn't feel there was an intense effort occurring.

There was only one event that was somewhat unusual. One afternoon I was brought into a room with a doctor and seven student doctors–at least I thought they were student doctors. The doctor asked me if I was wearing briefs under the hospital gown. I said, "Yes." He asked me to take off the gown.

He then asked me to lift my left foot and hop on the right leg. Then on the other leg. "Gee, you do that well," he said. I think he was impressed by the amount of spring in my legs. He asked if hopping caused any pain. I said, "No."

He then said to the student doctors, "Notice how well-defined his muscles are."

I said, "My chiropractor gave me exercises to do. But the exercises don't stop my back from going out, and they aren't bringing my hips back into place." With that, my performance for the student doctors ended.

A few hours before my release from the hospital, a doctor came into my room to talk to me. He said, "We think there are too many people you work with that you don't like."

I had told them that I was unhappy with the chairman of the computerization committee and the new supervisor. I hadn't made it a point to mention I was well satisfied with all my other co-workers.

I was released on Saturday, July 9. It had been a 6-day stay. I never got any additional communications from UW Hospital regarding the tests and examinations they had done, possibly because I wasn't the one paying the bill.

Overall, I thought the doctors at UW Hospital did well. They didn't subject me to another EMG test. (Sometimes less is better.) More important, they didn't give me any off-the-wall recommendations like the doctors I had been seeing.

As had been previously arranged, my 30-day leave of absence started with my return from the UW Hospital. I tried to put the time to good use.

The doctors at UW Hospital did find I had one inappropriate medical condition: excessive ear wax in one ear. But they didn't clean it.

I scheduled an appointment with Dr. Ray, the general practitioner, to have it cleaned. He had last seen me before I had chiropractic treatments. He was in his office when I arrived, and I made it a point to work briskly.

"What did you do to solve your back problem?" he asked.

"Four months of chiropractic treatment," I replied.

"Myself, I would never go to a chiropractor," he said.

I couldn't believe it. Here was a doctor who had seen me at my worst, couldn't help me, sees me as a recovered person, and yet wouldn't consider the method I used to recover.

What a dummy.

I used the 30 days to start looking for a new job–even though I wasn't sure I was going to resign from the Wisconsin Electric Power Co. I had drifted back into "undecided" about resigning.

Also, I used the 30 days to try biofeedback to resolve my back problem. I spent about six sessions hooked up to some electronic device and trying, via my mental processes, to make a beeping sound get louder, or maybe it was softer. I wasn't impressed by the technique and didn't see it as a way to solve my problem.

Finally, I got in a good amount of tennis during the 30 days.

My hips stayed misaligned during the 30 days. But I didn't have any other back problems.

My leave of absence ended on August 15. As I walked into the office that morning, one of my co-workers asked me, "Are you going to resign, or are you here to work?"

I said, "I don't know."

I checked into my supervisor's office, and he asked me the same question. I said, "I'm here to work." The workday passed without any significant events.

I belonged to a ski club, and during summers the club sponsored social tennis nights. It was easy, not-too-competitive tennis. On the night of August 15, I attended one of those events.

Everyone played doubles tennis, and we changed partners every set. I had been a winner in the first set, and my partner and I took a 4 - 1 lead in the second set.

A ball was hit a few steps to the right of me, and I started to run to hit it back. I suddenly realized that I could no longer run. All I could do was take steps. As play was going on, I tried to see if I could run. There was no question about it. My muscles, presumably my back muscles, had tightened so much I couldn't run.

That ended my "undecided" status about resigning. I had just finished a 30-day leave without back problems. On the night of my first day back at work, I find I can't run.

I went into work the next morning, submitted my letter of resignation, packed my personal items, and by noon I had left the Company. This time my resignation–dated 8-16-77–held.

Back at home that afternoon I reflected on my situation. I had just resigned from a job I liked and had held for 16 years. I was now unemployed. But I was happy, because I felt I had finally resolved my back problem. I figured it would take about a month for my back to return to normal.

I thought I ought to do something special to mark the occasion. The ceilings in my house were 8 feet high. I thought I ought to jump up and touch the ceiling simultaneously with both hands. I'm 5' 9". That meant I had to jump straight up a little over a foot. I was 39 years old at the time.

"Gosh," I thought, "Someone with a bad back shouldn't be doing that kind of jumping." I jumped and touched both hands to the ceiling. Then I did it a second time, just to prove I could.

I didn't sleep all that well that night. With my resignation finally accomplished, I had expected to sleep better.

Regardless, I felt I was moving to an improved life, and I started the next day with enthusiasm.

Due to my back problem, I hadn't been mowing my lawn. The grass and weeds were more than a foot high. I had gotten a notice from the city stating they would clean up my yard if I didn't. So my first activity was to cut the grass. By midafternoon, I had my yard in shipshape condition.

During the first week after my resignation, my hips moved in 1/4 inch. That meant my hips were still misaligned by 3/4 inch. Also I felt a little stronger. My sleeping improved only a minimal amount.

Prior to my August 16 resignation, I had considerable time off work: 3 weeks of vacation, 6 days at UW Hospital and a 30-day leave of absence. During that time-off period, my problem of being slightly incontinent stopped, and it would never return.

Similarly, the pain in the tip of my penis subsided. I dropped it off my mental list of items to monitor. Although it took several years, the problem eventually disappeared completely.

When I left home after graduating from high school, my mother and I started a practice of writing letters to each other. She wrote every week. I wrote every one to three weeks. We almost never talked on the phone.

I wrote her that I had resigned from my job. Two days later, I got a phone call from her. She said, "How could you quit such a good job?"

I spent the first few weeks following my resignation playing tennis. I planned on getting a job again after I had recovered from my back and sleeping problems.

I thought, "Everything seems to be looking good."

Chapter 06 A NEW JOB

After a month of unemployment, I realized my recovery had plateaued. Ninety per cent of my recovery had occurred in the first week after my resignation. My back had gone out once during the month. Previously my back had been going out every 10 - 14 days.

My improvement was enough to confirm that I had definitely made the right decision to resign. However, my recovery was far short of what I had expected.

I was getting tired of playing tennis, and I didn't like the idea of being unemployed. I decided to get a job and do it quickly. I applied in person for a programmer job at a Milwaukee software firm called the DASD Corporation. I was asked to take a programmer test, and I did. They told me I had correctly answered all the math questions on the test. They hired me on the spot and told me my first assignment would be a 6-week project in Los Angeles.

To a Wisconsinite, the idea of working in California had lots of appeal. My only concern was whether I could find the right chiropractor if my back went out. I had learned during my two years of chiropractic treatment that not all chiropractors could adjust me successfully.

On Sunday, September 18, 1977, three other DASD employees and I flew to Los Angeles. The motel, rental car, office facility, etc. all checked out fine—with one exception. We would be working the midnight shift, due to limited computer capacity during the day. What a bummer.

We took it easy that first week in Los Angeles. We worked 8-hour days. On the weekend, we took in Disneyland.

Early in the second week, we realized we wouldn't be able to complete the project in six weeks if we only worked eight hours a day. The project leader wanted everyone to work 10 hours a day and 7 days a week. I said I'd be willing to work 7 days a week, but a maximum of 9 hours a day—and on the day shift. He agreed to let me do that.

With my switch to the day shift, I started enjoying my daily routine. The work was interesting. (I was doing assembler language programming.) I used the nights to go shopping and to check out some of the nightspots in Los Angeles.

It was hot during the day. But in the evenings it cooled off, and I really enjoyed the warm, dry air.

We completed the project in just a little over 6 weeks, and I arrived back in Milwaukee on November 2. Five days after I returned, my back went out. My back hadn't gone out while I was in Los Angeles. I was pleased it had held until I got back to Milwaukee and could see my regular chiropractor.

Chapter 07 A JOB AT MANPOWER, INC.

After the midnight shifts and 7-day work weeks in Los Angeles, I knew I needed to find a different employer.

I sent my resume to various employers and got an interview with Manpower, Inc.

"What is your normal workday?" I asked.

"8 to 5," the manager said.

"How much overtime do you normally work?"

"We rarely work overtime," the manager said.

It definitely sounded like my kind of company.

On December 5, 1977, I started employment as a systems analyst in the corporate headquarters for Manpower, Inc. The headquarters was located about 5 miles from downtown Milwaukee. The job checked out well, and I decided I would definitely be with the Company for quite awhile. (I was with the DASD Corporation only three months.)

My first assignment was to assist in the installation of an accounts payable "package"–i.e., a computer software system. Later I was given full responsibility for the accounts payable system.

In March 1978, seven months after I resigned from Wisconsin Electric, I missed two days of work due to my back going out. It was a significant event. It was the first time I'd missed any days of work in half a year. In comparison, I'd missed work my last year at Wisconsin Electric almost every month because of back problems.

The next year (April 1978 to March 1979) was a stable period for me. My work activities at Manpower went smoothly. My health problems continued, but they were at a more acceptable level. My hips were still misaligned 3/4 inch, and my strength was still below normal. My back didn't go out nearly as often. The time between chiropractor visits ranged from 4 to 8 weeks. When my back did go out, it was no longer painful. It was comparable to a mild headache. My sleeping remained so-so. I would wake up once or twice each night, and sometimes I woke early. About once a week, I used Valium to get to sleep.

The 3/4-inch hip misalignment didn't cause any major problems. When I was occupied at work, etc., I wouldn't even sense the misalignment. However in the evening when I took walks, I was aware that my parts weren't all in their proper places. I didn't like it.

In April 1979, I decided it was time to leave Manpower, Inc., and I started circulating my resume.

When I left the Wisconsin Electric Power Co., I decided I wouldn't work for any company located within 6 blocks of the headquarters building in which I formerly worked. I had left the Company under unusual circumstances, and I thought "leaving some space" would be a good idea.

In May 1979, I received a job offer from an insurance company that was located in downtown Milwaukee–about 8 blocks from my former workplace. The insurance job looked good, and it also met my location requirement. On May 9, I accepted the job offer.

The next day, May 10, my back kicked out. I saw my chiropractor, but his adjustment didn't help much.

On Saturday, May 12, I saw my chiropractor again. My condition still didn't improve.

By Sunday, May 13, I was beginning to see the picture. My back normally improved the same day I saw the chiropractor. This time my back hadn't improved after two adjustments. That meant there was an external event causing the muscles to stay in spasm.

I had successfully accepted job offers from the DASD Corporation and Manpower, Inc. So I knew the stress involved in accepting the job was not the problem. I decided the work location was the problem–too close to the Wisconsin Electric Power Co. Furthermore, that meant all of the downtown Milwaukee companies were off-limits to me in terms of employment.

The next morning I called the insurance company and declined the job. I saw my chiropractor again, and this time my back returned to normal. At least, it returned to what was normal for me.

I stopped my job hunt. I decided I should stay at Manpower until I could sort out my new psychological problem with downtown Milwaukee.

Chapter 08 CALIFORNIA DREAMING

By now I was well aware that I could improve my health by changing my environment. My resignation from Wisconsin Electric had clearly demonstrated that. The insurance job episode triggered lots of new thinking along those lines.

Just the idea of working in downtown Milwaukee had caused my back to go out. In contrast to that, I remembered that I had no back problems during my 6-plus weeks in Los Angeles. Also, my back had gone out just 5 days after I returned from Los Angeles–i.e., no problem in Los Angeles, but a flare-up in Milwaukee. Maybe I could resolve my back (and sleeping) problems by moving to California.

At this time, my health problems were "moderate." I weighed leaving my roots against possible health improvements. I decided I should take the bold step.

In July 1979, I proceeded to try for a job in San Diego. I had once been in San Diego on vacation and had liked the city.

Things didn't go well. First I sent my resume to San Diego Gas and Electric. They never replied.

Then I tried working through an employment agency. They located a software company that was interested in me. However, my experience with the DASD Corporation made me want to shy away from software firms. In general, I wasn't getting much response to my resume.

I wasn't doing well either. Mainly the job search was causing me to be tense and sleep poorly. Since I was so uncomfortable, I thought I was probably pursuing the wrong objective. Ever since my resignation from the Wisconsin Electric Power Co., I had become very sensitive to my bodily reactions to plans, decisions, etc.

After just a 2-month effort, I stopped my search for a job in California. (Initially I had concentrated on San Diego, but later I told the employment agency to also consider Los Angeles.)

I was disturbed by what had occurred. I felt I had correctly identified California as the solution to my health problems. Yet when I had tried for a California job, I had suffered significant tension and insomnia. In short, I wasn't able to accomplish the move to California.

Chapter 09 MORE JOB CHANGES

In November 1979, three months after I stopped my California job search, I resumed my job hunt. Only this time I decided to get a job at a utility. I had already checked out all the utility companies in Wisconsin, and none had appealed to me. I decided my goal was a utility out of state, but in the Midwest.

My approach was probably a little different than the one most people would use. I took a 3-day trip and visited each of the Midwest utilities that interested me. I visited the headquarters of utilities in Indianapolis, IN; Columbus, OH; Toledo, OH and Louisville, KY. (Louisville wasn't exactly Midwestern, but it was close enough.) I checked out each city. I tried to get a feel for each company based on how its headquarters building was designed, maintained, located, etc.

I returned home from my trip at 9:00 p.m. on November 4. One hour later, my back went out. It seemed like I just couldn't make any progress on finding a new job.

I drove back to Indianapolis two weeks later to check out the Indianapolis Power and Light Co. a second time. From my perspective, I thought it was the best of the batch. When I returned home, the result was the same. My back went out.

Undaunted, I filled out a job application for the Indianapolis Power and Light Co. I followed up my application with a phone call two weeks later. But I never heard from the Company.

I'm not sure what prompted it, but in January 1980 I started applying for various government jobs.

On February 6, I had a job interview for a position at the city of Madison. It was a small shop, maybe ten programmers and analysts. I had the interview at 6:00 p.m. Only the supervisor and I were in the office, and I asked him to show me around the work area. The computer staff was using just two rooms. It looked like the job was a good fit for me.

On the following Monday, I was offered the Madison job. I said I'd give my answer within two days. As I reviewed the situation in my mind, I remembered that I had seen radios on the desks of some of the employees. Somehow the significance of those radios hadn't hit me when I first saw them.

I can't stand radios at work. We had Muzak at Manpower and the Wisconsin Electric Power Co. It played for 15 minutes, and then there was 15 minutes of quiet. It wasn't too loud, and I was able to shut it out.

I called the supervisor at Madison and got some additional information on the radios. "No," he said, "They're not just for Saturdays and overtime hours. There's usually at least one radio playing all day." I declined the job.

In late February, I got a job interview at the University of Wisconsin-Milwaukee (UWM), and they offered me a systems analyst job. I accepted. The University is located roughly 3 miles from downtown Milwaukee.

My last day at Manpower was March 13, 1980. I had worked for them a little over two years. My main accomplishment for the Company was the installation, and extensive modification, of an accounts payable software package. The accounts payable system was running smoothly when I left.

I was also involved in a couple of other projects at Manpower. I wrote a badly-needed print utility computer program. I did some programming for an IBM Series 1 computer, using a language called Champtalk. (My job title was systems analyst. However, I did both systems analysis and programming work.)

I learned structured computer programming while I was at Manpower. Structured programming was just coming into general use during that time period.

Although Manpower didn't fit into my long-range plans, I enjoyed my work assignments there.

Finally, the Company held a one-day tennis tournament in June 1978, and I won it. The draw wasn't that big, but the trophy was huge.

I started work at UWM on March 17, 1980. My first day at work was good. After that, my UWM job started going downhill.

I had spent four years in college, and I had enjoyed the college environment. But as I spent my first few days as a systems analyst at the University, I kept thinking of that saying, "You can never go back."

I was now 42 years old, and the college culture no longer appealed to me. I didn't get any warm and fuzzy feeling as I walked around campus. More important, I wasn't impressed with how business was conducted at my new shop. In short, the managers and systems analysts at the University didn't work in the way that I'd known in the business world.

After a month at the University, I decided that accepting the position had been a mistake. I contacted an employment agency, and—once again—I got my resume circulating.

During July and August 1980, my job search went to a feverish pitch. I had decided to bring California back into the picture. (I still thought that a move to California could resolve my health problems.) I was using a Wisconsin employment agency, a California employment agency and also sending out resumes myself.

In Wisconsin, there was activity involving Milwaukee County, Kohl's, State of Wisconsin and MGIC. I had at least one interview at each of the organizations.

In California, there was activity involving San Diego County, City of San Jose, Sacramento County, San Diego Unified School District and Safeway Stores. My interviews with San Diego County and the City of San Jose were scheduled for the first week in September.

While all this job hunting was going on, I was in turmoil. I couldn't decide if I should get a Wisconsin job or a California job. I knew it was not a decision I would make on an intellectual level. My emotional side would make the decision. I seemed to be leaning to California.

From a health viewpoint, I wasn't doing too well. My use of Valium was increasing. My back was going out a lot.

On August 26, 1980, I had a pre-employment physical exam at Milwaukee County, and they offered me a systems analyst job. That evening my back went out.

On August 28, I had a job interview in Madison with the State of Wisconsin. The next day my back went out.

On August 31, the day before I was to fly to California, my back went out. That incident was particularly troubling for me. I was using these "back out" incidents as signs of which jobs were emotionally acceptable—i.e., the "back out" meant a job was unacceptable. The back problems on August 26 and 28 meant those jobs were unacceptable. I was concerned that my back problem on August 31 meant that California jobs were also unacceptable.

On September 1, I flew to San Diego for the first of two interviews in California. I arrived in San Diego early in the afternoon and immediately drove to the San Diego County headquarters building–to get a feel for the County.

I saw a huge, 4-story, stucco building with a big courtyard entrance. Large areas of well-maintained lawn surrounded the building. Parking lots for hundreds of cars were located to the north and south of the building. The building, lawn and parking lots took up an extensive area–one city block wide and about two blocks long. Located about 100 yards west of the building was the ocean–more precisely, San Diego Bay. I liked what I saw.

I had my job interview at 9:00 a.m. the next day. I sat on a chair in an open area in the middle of the room. Three people seated behind a table asked questions. The interview lasted 30 minutes, maybe a little longer. I thought I did okay in the interview, but I didn't feel like I was a shoo-in for the job.

I asked to be shown through the work area. The analysts were working in the basement, and their cubicles were really small–i.e., the inside of the building was not as impressive as the outside.

I was told that the County of San Diego had 16,000 employees. (In comparison, Wisconsin Electric had slightly over 4,000 employees when I resigned in 1977.)

When I was ready to leave, the supervisor handling interviews said, "Call me on Friday. I'll let you know our decision." My experience was that when an offer to hire someone is made, usually the company (or the employment agency) contacts the applicant. Since this was the reverse, I felt my chances were not good.

I spent the rest of the day checking out San Diego. I expected the homes to be expensive, and they were. What surprised me was the flimsy construction. Some of the yards consisted of stones and rocks–not something to warm the heart of a Midwesterner. (Later I learned that the use of stones and rocks for yards wasn't particularly common.)

I was impressed with the clerks and servers in motels, restaurants, etc. They were good-looking and sharp.

I hardly need to mention how nice the city itself looked—clean homes and streets, more trees than I had expected, some big parks, many bays and exciting, uneven terrain. (San Diego has lots of canyons.)

Next I flew to Oakland, California. I had been considering a job in the Oakland area, and I wanted to check out the city. I spent half a day in Oakland and then drove to San Jose.

I had an interview at the City of San Jose on September 5. I had a one-on-one interview with a first-line supervisor. He then had me talk to the manager. The interview with the manager didn't go well. He was polite, but I knew at the end of the conversation I would never hear from him again. And I didn't.

My flight home was from the San Francisco airport. Just before my flight left, I called to check on the San Diego job.

"We'd like to offer you the job of systems analyst," he said.

"Oh, I know my answer right now," I said, "But I'll call and give you my confirmation on Monday."

I remember hanging up the pay phone receiver and saying out loud, "Oh my, oh my, oh my." I was very, very pleased—and surprised.

The following Monday I accepted the San Diego position, with September 29 to be my first day of work.

I owned my home. So I then set about the tasks to rent out my house and move to San Diego. My plan was to spend a minimum of one year in San Diego. If things didn't work out, I could easily return to my home in Milwaukee.

By 10:00 a.m. on September 21, I had loaded my car and an attached U-HAUL trailer with the furniture, clothing, etc. that I would be taking with me. I left for California.

I had gone from September 1 to September 21 without my back kicking out even once. (My back would not go out again in the next nine months.)

Chapter 10 THE CALIFORNIA CURE

I had accepted a systems analyst position at both the County of Milwaukee and the County of San Diego. The starting date for the Milwaukee job was September 22.

I had kept both options open. On the night of the first day of my drive to San Diego, I mailed a letter to the County of Milwaukee stating I was declining the job. I mailed the letter from Missouri. In those days the postal service still collected mail on Sundays. There was a slight chance they would receive the letter on my scheduled starting date.

My drive to San Diego was without incident, with one exception. As I was driving through the desert in Arizona, I pulled into a rest stop. Just after I had gotten out of my car, a man came up to me and asked if I had jumper cables. He said his truck wouldn't start. I looked and the only truck around was an 18-wheeler. He said he had a battery. He just needed cables.

We were somewhere in the middle of the desert. So I gave him my cables. He and his partner got the 18-wheeler started.

He handed my jumper cables back to me. The cable clamps had been melted. I said, "You ruined my cables."

He said, "How much did you pay for them?"

"15 dollars."

He pulled out his wallet and said, "All I have is a $20 bill. Do you have 5 dollars?"

I took the $20 bill and gave him a $5 bill.

Things didn't jibe. I would think an 18-wheeler would carry jumper cables. For starting an 18-wheeler in the middle of a desert, you ought to be given a $20 bill—maybe a couple.

I never had any further contact with the men and the 18-wheeler.

I arrived in San Diego on September 25, 1980. It was early afternoon. Next to a downtown bank, I found two metered parking spaces for my car and U-HAUL trailer. I planned to open a checking account and rent a safe deposit box.

During the preparations and drive to San Diego, I had no concerns about the choice I had made. There were no second thoughts. There had been no sadness when I left Wisconsin. However as I sat in my car outside that bank, I did have a few minutes of doubt. "Man," I thought, "What have I done?"

It disturbed me that I didn't have an apartment or house. I didn't know anyone in San Diego—not a soul. The doubts didn't last long. I took care of my banking business.

It's tough to rent an apartment in a strange city, especially if you're driving around with a U-HAUL trailer attached to your car. I rented an apartment my second day in San Diego, and I went through the usual routines of settling in. I was feeling comfortable.

Chapter 11 A COUNTY JOB

On September 29, 1980, I reported for my first day of work at the County of San Diego. I spent the first couple hours filling out payroll forms, and then I was introduced to my new supervisor.

My supervisor led me to the work area and pointed out the cubicle assigned to me. I had been concerned about the size of cubicles. The cubicle assigned to me was 50% larger than any of the others in the area. What a nice plus!

My supervisor then spent most of the day showing me around the office, explaining work activities, etc. He showed me a sheet of computer printout. He said, "We have an IBM 3800 laser printer. It prints 215 pages a minute and prints on 8½ by 11-inch paper." At the time, laser printers were just coming into widespread use. I had read about laser printers, but had never seen one. San Diego County was looking very good to me.

On day two that changed. As I walked to my desk, I hear a radio playing in one of the cubicles in my work area–definitely a downer for me. About 11:00 a.m. I heard a second radio. At this point I was on super alert for radio sounds. And I picked up the sound from yet a third radio, located on the other side of a "divider wall." "Oh, no," I thought. I was devastated.

The County had flextime. Some employees worked "9 by 9" – 9 hours a day, 9 days every two weeks and one workday off. The employees who owned the radios had been off my first day at work.

The department had very few meeting rooms. So I had my supervisor step out of the building for a meeting. "Say," I said, "There's one heck of a lot of radios playing in our area. Does the department have any rules on radios?"

"Well, employees are allowed to play them. Once we even had a woman playing opera music. And it was loud," he said.

The next day I called in sick–because I was sick. I knew I couldn't adjust to those radios. Just seven months earlier I had declined the job at the city of Madison because of radios.

That afternoon I went to an employment agency. I explained my plight, and asked the recruiter to circulate my resume. He suggested I play my own radio at work.

I followed the recruiter's advice. It worked fairly well. I wasn't interested in listening to music from my radio, but it did drown out the other radios. In case you've lost count, we now had four radios playing simultaneously.

I had made the move to California, but I hadn't found happiness.

Chapter 12 CALIFORNIA – THE FIRST 6 MONTHS

From a health viewpoint, my move to California was successful. My back didn't kick out at all during the first six months. During that period, my hips shifted left 1/4 inch–certainly a noteworthy improvement. And with that improvement, my hips were now misaligned only ½ inch.

I started to sleep just a little better. However, I continued to use Valium about twice a week for sleeping purposes.

At work I was getting interesting assignments. Just like at Manpower, I worked on the Accounts Payable System. I had both systems analysis and programming projects, with the programming being done in COBOL.

My second week in California, I picked up a list showing the location of all the tennis courts in San Diego. I drove to each location. It didn't take much effort to decide that Morley Field, which has 25 courts and is located in Balboa Park, was the best of the lot. It was easy to get pickup games, and I was at the courts almost every weekend.

The radio problem at work improved moderately. My supervisor got one of the analysts to use a headset to listen to his radio. But it was still a problem I had to resolve.

So I was once again circulating my resume and doing job interviews. I had a job interview within three weeks of my arrival in San Diego. I got a fair number of interviews. However, the jobs for which I was interviewing weren't as good as the County job I already had.

I considered leaving San Diego. I even considered leaving California. I thought Oregon or Washington looked like reasonable alternatives.

And I definitely considered moving back to Milwaukee. However, my gut feeling was that I couldn't move back. I had made it a point to keep my Milwaukee home so I could easily move back, but I considered that an unworkable strategy.

My third weekend in San Diego, I happened to turn on the TV and caught a Milwaukee Bucks basketball game in progress. I wasn't a Bucks fan, but I knew the names of the star players. It was a connection to "back home," and I left the game on. After watching the game 5 to 10 minutes, I started feeling sick–and I don't mean homesick. I realized the game on TV was the cause. I turned off the TV.

Many things were going well for me in San Diego, but the radio problem remained.

Chapter 13 MORE SURPRISES

In June 1981, my back went out on me–the first time in 9 months. So I guess you could call it a surprise. It wasn't just a 24-hour problem. I was off work a full week. I selected a chiropractor, Dr. William, from the yellow pages. Luckily I got a good one. I even talked him into treating me on a Saturday, a day his office was normally closed.

After that one-full-week problem, my back returned to its old ways. Once a month or so, my back would go out. If I got chiropractic treatment quickly, the whole incident–from onset to recovery–took 24 hours. The discomfort involved was normally minor, and it seldom resulted in me missing a day of work.

September 25, 1981, marked my 1-year anniversary in California. I hadn't been back to Wisconsin, and I decided it was time to take a vacation there. I called one of the airlines and made a reservation.

Boy, did I get a surprise! I started getting slight shots of pain in my back. The muscles in my body got tight, and my eyesight got poorer. (Poorer eyesight had long been the first sign that my back was going out.)

I was so tense I couldn't stand it. I cancelled my flight reservation. And all returned to normal.

The incident scared me. I was already pretty sure that I couldn't permanently return to Wisconsin, and I was willing to accept that. But just taking a vacation there was another matter.

I tried a few more times to fly to Wisconsin. Each time I got so tense I had to cancel the reservation. I decided to get "professional help." I had been in psychotherapy for about a year when I was in college. So I knew psychotherapy–i.e., talk therapy–wouldn't be of any help.

When I was 29 years old, I had once solved a problem using hypnosis. I decided to try hypnosis again.

Soon I was seeing a psychologist who used hypnosis as his basic technique. In the first session, he hypnotized me and suggested that my left arm would rise on its own. I'll be darned. It did. (This raising of the arm is a standard technique in hypnosis. But this was the first time it had ever been done to me.) He then suggested that for "yes" answers the index finger would raise itself, and for "no" answers the middle finger would raise itself.

Each session followed the same format. For the first 10 minutes, I would discuss with him subjects that I thought should be investigated, and I would give him background information.

He would then hypnotize me. Next he would ask a question, and the index or middle finger would raise itself to provide the answer. (I never felt that I was consciously controlling and raising the finger.)

For example, he might ask, "Is that payroll-personnel computerization project an ongoing source of anxiety?"

Assume that the index finger raised itself to signify a "yes" answer.

He would then say something like, "Is the subconscious mind willing to reconcile and remove those anxieties now?"

Assume the index finger raised itself.

"Would the subconscious please do that reconciliation now and raise the index finger when the reconciliation has been completed."

Within about five seconds, the index finger would raise itself.

The goal was to remove anxieties to a point where I would be able to take a vacation in Wisconsin.

I had put my house in Milwaukee up for sale, and I got an "offer to purchase" in October 1981. I accepted the offer. (In this book, I refer to my home as a "Milwaukee house." More precisely, my home was located in Shorewood, a suburb of Milwaukee.)

I needed to go back to complete the house sale. I had left appliances at the house, and they also needed to be sold.

I had now been in hypnosis sessions once or twice a week for two months. But I still couldn't return to Wisconsin.

I continued the hypnosis for another month, and the date for the closing on my house was near. Then one day in a hypnosis session, we determined that I could return to Wisconsin. I made my flight reservation that very night. And I felt relaxed.

I flew to Wisconsin on December 3, 1981, and spent the next three weeks there. First I took care of the main item: I sold the house (and appliances). Then I spent the rest of the time visiting family and friends, playing tennis, etc. It was an excellent vacation.

I thought the hypnosis had not been a factor in my being able to return to Wisconsin. I felt strongly about my home in Milwaukee. It was like a magnet for me. I think my subconscious decided it would allow me to go to Wisconsin to get rid of the magnet.

Even though I had misgivings about the hypnosis, I continued my hypnosis sessions when I returned from Wisconsin. I still had a radio problem at work, and I needed to find a new place of employment. I thought that a Wisconsin job was still my best bet, even though I had just sold my Milwaukee home. To accomplish that, I needed some kind of psychological breakthrough. I hoped that hypnosis would provide it.

I continued with hypnosis on a once or twice a week basis until April 1982. (I had started in September 1981.) In the last two months, the psychologist began deviating from the format we had initially adopted. In the end he was trying to cast out demons, and I thought it was getting silly. I thought the 8 months of hypnosis had been a waste of time.

Chapter 14 POSSIBLE RETURN TO WISCONSIN ELECTRIC

In September 1982, I phoned one of my former co-workers at the Wisconsin Electric Power Co. I was looking for the latest news, gossip, etc. I got unexpected news. I was told that the chairman of the payroll-personnel computerization committee had passed away. He died of a heart attack. I always thought he was about 3 years younger than me. That meant he died at about age 41.

The payroll-personnel computer project had been cancelled some time earlier, and he had been assigned other duties.

I had always considered that project–and maybe the project leader–as a possible cause of my back problem. Since the project and the project leader no longer existed, I thought I might be able to return to the Wisconsin Electric Power Co.

For about a week, I thought about returning to the Company. My bodily reactions were not positive. I started feeling tense and the quality of my sleep went down.

I dropped the idea.

Chapter 15 A BANK JOB

After numerous job interviews that went nowhere, I finally got an interview–in October 1982–that I thought had possibilities. It was at the San Diego Trust and Savings Bank.

Banks are notorious for non-stop music, and I was on the alert for it. I was interviewed twice, on different days, at the bank's data processing center. I didn't hear one note of music.

I was offered the bank job and I accepted.

I gave 2-weeks notice to my manager at the County. In early 1982, I had been transferred to the group responsible for maintaining the payroll computer programs, and it had been at the behest of the payroll group manager. His name was Lawrence.

Lawrence tried to talk me out of resigning. I didn't tell him why I was leaving, but I stated I was going to take the new job. (My dislike, even abhorrence, for radios at work wasn't common knowledge.)

On November 18, 1982, I reported for my first day of work at the San Diego Trust and Savings Bank. I reported to the personnel area in the data processing center. I stepped into the room, and the first sound I heard was music from built-in speakers. "Oh boy," I thought, "I hope this is just in the personnel area."

Next I was escorted to the analysts area, where I had been interviewed. I was greeted by more music. I think I was greeted by some people too. But all I can remember is the music.

It didn't take long, and I was in conference with my new supervisor. "Say," I said, "I don't remember any music in your office the last time I was here."

"I often turn off the music in here," he said.

"Do you also control the speakers in the hallways?" (There was no music in the hallways on the days I interviewed.)

"No, I don't know where that control is."

The offices for analysts were well-constructed, with permanent floor-to-ceiling walls—i.e., not cubicles. There were two analysts to an office. In order to work without music, I would have to persuade the analyst working with me to turn off the speaker in the room. Then to shut out the music from the hallway speakers, the door to the office would have to be kept closed. I didn't think I could pull that off.

"What a disaster," I thought.

Yes, the music had been turned off in the room where I had been interviewed. But how could I have missed all the other music?

Incidentally, I made it a point not to ask about radios and music during interviews. I had once done it in an interview, and it had been a definite turn-off.

I decided I'd better get back to the County job. I called Lawrence and explained my situation. He was receptive to me returning, but he said he'd have to talk to the department director. The next day (Friday), Lawrence called me and told me I was to meet with the director on Monday.

Monday at 8:00 a.m., I met with the director. It wasn't a meeting with a lot of discussion. I'm sure she had already made her decision before the meeting. She told me I could report back to work at the County the next day.

On November 23, 1982, I was back in my old cubicle at the County. And happy to be there! I had missed three workdays due to my employment at the bank.

The bank experience settled the job change issue for me. I decided I would stay with the County. And that decision held. During the next 17 years I would not circulate my resume or have any job interviews.

Now let me dispose of the radio issue. There was one radio in our payroll group area, and Lawrence took care of it. I would spend the next four years in that physical area.

In September 1986, I was assigned to work on a new jail management computer system. That assignment required me—over a period of years—to move to a couple of different work locations. There were no radios at any of the locations.

In 1990, there was an extensive relocating of analysts. I saw that there would be a problem, because one woman always played a radio all day long. I talked to the manager in charge of the move and asked that the woman and her radio be put on one end of the room and I, on the other end. The manager agreed.

So I was always concerned about potential radio problems, but I never had any actual radio problems after 1982.

In general I'm very sensitive to noise. However, I never had problems with the noise and sounds that one normally encounters in an office—except for radios.

Finally, I do sometimes listen to radio music during my off-work hours. But usually I play a compact disc on a boom box.

Chapter 16 THE YEARS 1983 AND 1984

After deciding in late 1982 to stay with the County and having the radios issue basically solved, I settled down somewhat.

Throughout 1983 and 1984, my health status remained at a fairly constant–and reasonably acceptable–level. There were, however, two problems that continued to bother me. I had a fear of utilities and of Wisconsin.

My fear of utilities was now well established. However, as long as I didn't apply for a utility job, the fear didn't create any problems.

With regard to my fear of Wisconsin, the scope of my problem had changed. When I was living in Wisconsin, I considered downtown Milwaukee–where my former employer was located–to be a problem. Now that I lived in California, my problem had expanded to include the entire state of Wisconsin.

That fear of Wisconsin was creating a significant problem: I couldn't fly back to Wisconsin to see my immediate family, relatives, friends, etc.

Whenever I made a plane reservation to fly to Wisconsin, I would get so tense I couldn't stand it. I would cancel the reservation, usually the day after I made the reservation. (This was occurring even though I had successfully flown to Wisconsin to sell my home in December 1981.) Once I cancelled the plane reservation, my tension level would return to normal.

So once again, I tried hypnosis as a means of overcoming my fear of Wisconsin. There was, after all, some possibility that hypnosis had helped me to fly back in December 1981.

I saw the hypnotist approximately once a week for three months (May - July 1983). It didn't have any effect. I stopped my sessions with him, and then didn't pursue any treatment for about a year.

In May 1984, I tried hypnosis again. This time the hypnotist was a psychiatrist. In addition to the hypnosis, he prescribed Tofranil, which is a medicine for depression.

He thought I was depressed. I didn't think I was. Right from the start, Tofranil gave me a spaced-out feeling. I felt like I wasn't in contact with the people and things around me. Tofranil also increased my appetite tremendously—about a 150% increase. At a fast food restaurant, I never used to order more than one hamburger. Tofranil changed that. I started ordering two hamburgers and felt like that might not be enough.

He was treating me for a disease I didn't think I had. Regardless, the treatment was worse than the disease. After maybe a week, I quit taking Tofranil.

I don't know if Tofranil would have been able to end my so-called depression. I do know that Tofranil would have ended my days as an athlete with fast feet.

When he prescribed the medicine, the psychiatrist told me it might cause "dry mouth," and that I should drink a little more water. He didn't mention the really bad side effects. I wasn't impressed with how he'd handled the matter.

After seeing the psychiatrist for two months, I stopped treatment. The hypnosis wasn't any better than the Tofranil.

I had read that acupuncture could help some anxiety and insomnia problems. In July 1984, I gave acupuncture a try. My acupuncturist, Dr. Vinh, was a regular medical doctor. As part of his initial contact with me, he took my blood pressure. It was 135/90. He said, "Your blood pressure is a little high. I don't know how much I can help your insomnia, but I can help you on the blood pressure."

I said, "Any help will be appreciated." I knew my blood pressure was borderline high. I had been advised by another doctor to take a diuretic drug to lower my blood pressure. I had declined to take the drug, because I thought my blood pressure was still within an acceptable normal range.

I asked the acupuncturist, "What am I suppose to do during this acupuncture treatment?"

"Nothing. Go to sleep."

I wasn't about to go to sleep with all those needles sticking in me. (However, I often did fall asleep during subsequent acupuncture treatments.)

I had roughly 20 needles sticking in me, and he left them in place for 20, maybe 30, minutes.

He removed the needles and took my blood pressure. It was 120/80. Perfect!

To finish this blood pressure subject, I found that in the next 17 years my blood pressure basically remained around the 120/80 readings. There were 4 or 5 times when my blood pressure went back into the borderline high range. So 4 or 5 times in the subsequent 17 years, I went back to see him. Each time he brought my blood pressure back to the 120/80 range–with one treatment.

Based on information provided by this one acupuncturist, the parameters for treating high blood pressure with acupuncture are as follows: If the patient has high blood pressure due to physical conditions (e.g., partially blocked arteries, etc.), acupuncture won't lower the blood pressure. If the patient has high blood pressure due to nervousness, acupuncture can lower the blood pressure.

With regard to treating me for anxiety and insomnia, the acupuncturist asked me to come back for three more treatments. I received those three acupuncture treatments, but there was no progress. So we stopped the treatments.

The years 1983 and 1984 weren't completely filled with fears and medical activities. In July 1983, my partner and I won the men's doubles (Class C) tennis tournament sponsored by the Balboa Tennis Club in San Diego.

Three months later, we made it to the finals–but lost–in the Griffin Tennis Tournament held at Grossmont College. I was 45 years old at the time.

Overall I was doing reasonably well.

Chapter 17 SELLING MY CAR

When I moved to San Diego in 1980, I was driving a 1977 Oldsmobile Cutlass Supreme. By 1984, it was showing wear and tear. So in November 1984, I ordered a new car from the factory–a 1985 Buick Regal. I took delivery of the car in late January 1985.

I advertised my 1977 Olds in a car-for-sale publication for $1,800. About a week later, a young fellow showed up at my apartment. He wanted to see the car.

The 1977 Olds had an emblem on the trunk that consisted of a car dealer's name and the word "Milwaukee." When the prospective buyer saw it, he said, "Hey, I'm from Wisconsin too." We talked a little about how long we had been living in California, etc.

He agreed to buy the car for $1,800, but he didn't have the full amount. He gave me $500 and said he'd have the rest in 10 days.

The next two days were not good days for me. I was feeling tense, I needed Valium to sleep, and I knew the problem was that the buyer was from Wisconsin. That fact was disturbing me.

On the third day, I woke in the middle of the night and the solution came to me. I should tell the buyer that the car had a bad transmission and that, as a fellow Wisconsinite, I wouldn't sell the car to him.

And that's exactly what I did. He reluctantly accepted his $500. He said, "You found someone who will give you $2,000 for that car."

That night I wrote in my diary: "Now I have to sell the car again. But I feel comfortable. The whole thing is, of course, very stupid. I should be able to sell my car to anyone–including a Wisconsinite."

Three weeks later I sold the car for $1,200. My fear of Wisconsin had cost me $600. In the coming years, it would cost me a lot more than that.

Chapter 18 BUYING GOLD RIMMED GLASSES

As I described in the preceding chapter, selling an item could be difficult for me. I was also having problems on the buying side.

Shortly after joining Manpower in December 1977, I decided I needed to replace my eyeglasses. I had an eye examination and picked out a pair of gold rimmed glasses.

When I put on my new glasses, I found I couldn't see very well. They didn't feel right. I went back to the optometrist and had them adjusted. They still weren't any good.

I decided to start over. I went to a different optical shop and purchased another pair of gold rimmed eyeglasses. They didn't work either.

Somehow I decided that maybe the gold rims were the problem. So next I bought rimless glasses. I even had the upper portion of the lenses tinted. (At the time, Rose Colored Glasses by John Conlee was a top country song.)

Using the rimless glasses, I found I could see "fine." My new glasses issue was settled.

In April 1983, I ordered gold rimmed glasses again. (I was now in California, and it had been over five years since I last tried gold rimmed glasses.) And again, I was unsuccessful. I felt so uncomfortable about the glasses that I cancelled the order before the frames even arrived.

In August 1983, I tried once more. Only this time I took delivery of the gold rimmed glasses. I put the glasses on at noon. As the afternoon went by, I could tell my back was going out. When I got home that evening, I threw away the glasses.

Finally in October 1989, I attempted again to wear gold rimmed glasses. In 1974, I had worn gold rimmed glasses, and I still had the 1974 pair in my possession. Of course, the frames had lost a little of their sparkle. I had the frames fitted according to my latest prescription. I picked up the frame with the new lenses on a

Saturday morning. That evening about 11:00 p.m., I threw away the glasses.

It would be more than a decade before I would try again.

Chapter 19 GOALS ACCOMPLISHED

I moved to California to solve a back problem. My hip misalignment improved 1/4 inch during my first six months in California. By 1985, my hips were back to their proper alignment– i.e., there had been an additional ½ inch improvement. To another person, that last ½ inch was imperceptible. But I saw it. And I saw when it was gone.

In other words, it took 10 years for the 4-inch hip misalignment I had in 1975 to correct itself.

In terms of strength, I'm not sure I ever fully regained my strength. However, by 1985 I had come pretty close. I moved several times in San Diego. I moved everything myself, except items that required two men–e.g., sofa, portable dish washer, etc.

There was one aspect of my back problem that wouldn't correct itself. My back kept going out. As I described earlier, there wasn't any pain involved. But I didn't feel well. It was the equivalent of having a mild headache. It occurred about once a month, based on statistics for the years 1983 and 1984.

In short, I had resolved the major aspects of my back problem, but some minor ones still remained.

I thought my back improved because I moved myself so far from the location of the Wisconsin Electric headquarters–i.e., ground zero for me. Fortunately I didn't have to leave the United States.

By 1985, I finally recognized that my move to California had solved another problem–my job problem. From 1977 to 1980, I had held three different jobs in Milwaukee, and I hadn't been completely satisfied with any of them. In contrast to that, I was well satisfied with my job at the County and was planning to be there a long time.

As I already described, my first year at the County wasn't all that great. However, after that things got better.

In 1983, I got a chance to be a project leader on a full life-cycle computer project–i.e., requirements study, design, programming and installation. It was called the Probation Accounting Computerization Project. I took a manual operation and turned it into a computerized operation.

It was a rare assignment. It's the only full life-cycle project I worked on during my entire career.

It took my team and me 2½ years to build and install the Probation Accounting Computer System. And that baby hummed.

Not too long after I completed the Probation Accounting Project in 1985, our department director was looking for an analyst to beef up a behind-schedule project to build a new jail management computer system. My manager recommended me.

When I was in college, I certainly never envisioned myself in a jail operation. But there I was: getting a tour of a San Diego County jail and gathering information for the new jail computer system.

The Detentions Processing Manager asked, "Do you know anything about jail systems?"

"No, but these computer systems are all similar. I'll be able to build it," I replied. In retrospect, even I'm surprised at the confidence in my statement. (Approximately two years later, we installed the new jail computer system.)

I would be involved in County jail computer systems for many years to come.

Regardless of my job and health accomplishments, I missed Wisconsin. I was isolated in California.

Chapter 20 THE 1985 FLIGHT

By August 1985, it had been almost 4 years since I had been in Wisconsin. I wanted to visit the people I knew there.

My parents were now in their seventies, and they had never flown. They said they wouldn't fly to California.

In late August, I phoned my sister to discuss an alternative plan. I suggested that she and her husband bring Mom and Dad to Nashville, Tennessee, and that I would fly out and meet them there. My sister agreed.

My plan had a flaw. I couldn't handle it. I got so tense I couldn't stand it. I phoned my sister and cancelled.

Some of you are probably thinking, "Why doesn't he just get on a plane and fly back—i.e., just do it."

Aha, I thought of that too. One day I was sitting in my apartment and I thought to myself, "God damn it. I'm going to fly back, and I'm going to do it today."

I thought, "I'll drive to the airport, get a ticket and fly out tonight." With a ticket in hand, cancelling the flight would be more difficult. By flying out the same day, I could avoid the "bad night of sleep."

Today the airlines almost require 7-day and 14-day advance purchases of tickets, and my plan might be unreasonable. But in 1985, the airlines had fewer restrictions on ticket purchases. You could pull off what I had in mind.

I was living on the upper level of a two-story apartment building. There was an outside stairway to the ground level. I grabbed my wallet and car keys, locked the apartment door and headed for the stairway. A man on a mission.

I got to the fourth step. Zingo, my back went out. I could still walk, but not very well. I decided that if I proceeded, the muscles in my back would lock up so tightly I wouldn't be able to move.

I never tried that tactic again.

When I was receiving acupuncture treatments from Dr. Vinh, he had made it clear that if there was no noticeable improvement in my insomnia after 3 or 4 treatments, there was no point in continuing. However, I thought acupuncture was the only avenue I had left for me to achieve some improvement in my anxiety and insomnia problems.

I went to another acupuncturist, Dr. Shen. The first treatment by him proceeded very well, and I found it particularly relaxing. After about 30 minutes of treatment, he removed the needles.

He then said, "I'm going to put a small pin in each ear. I want you to leave the pins in until your next treatment." He inserted the two pins. Oh, I didn't like it. The pins brought the tension right back. I didn't say anything.

Within a couple hours, my back went out. I knew I needed to get those pins removed. So that same day I went back to Dr. Shen's office. I told him the pins had caused my back to kick out and had him remove them. I showed him how my back and hips were misaligned, maybe 2 inches. (I don't know if he believed his pins had caused my back to go out.)

Even though the first treatment didn't go particularly well, Dr. Shen seemed like a very capable acupuncturist. I kept seeing Dr. Shen about once a week, on Saturdays, for acupuncture. I thought the acupuncture might be helping me a little on the anxiety and insomnia. On the other hand, it seemed like the acupuncture sometimes caused my back to go out. I was unsure on both issues.

On November 18, 1985, I started a 2-week vacation. Mainly it was to take some time off from work. I didn't have any activities planned. I spent the first three days playing tennis.

Then on the fourth day of my vacation, it happened. I was sitting in my apartment, and the thought occurred to me that I should fly to Wisconsin. And I felt like I could do it.

At 2:00 p.m. I phoned for a reservation. At 4:00 p.m. I took a taxi to the San Diego airport. At 5:30 p.m. I was on a plane headed for Chicago. What great airline service! And it didn't cost me an arm and a leg.

There was a layover in Denver. I phoned my sister, told her I would be at her house about 3:00 a.m., and asked her to leave the back door unlocked. I had deliberately not phoned her from San

Diego. I knew there was a possibility I might still change my mind in the middle of the flight.

At 3:30 a.m., I arrived at my sister's house. Oh, it was good to be back.

My stay in Wisconsin was for ten days. I visited lots of people, including some of my former co-workers at the Wisconsin Electric Power Co. I managed to squeeze in a date with a gal I had previously dated when I lived in Milwaukee.

My parents had purchased a new home in New Holstein, WI. And I got to see it for the first time.

I drove to lots of the spots that had been important to me. I spent my first two years in high school at Roosevelt Junior High School and Fond du Lac Senior High School in Fond du Lac, WI. (The names of the schools have since been changed.) So I made it a point to drive through the Fond du Lac area a couple of times. I spent my last two years in high school at Stockbridge High School in Stockbridge, WI. My parents and I visited the farm where we had lived, just a couple miles outside of Stockbridge. Finally, I checked on the house I used to own in Milwaukee.

To my delight, I had no back problems during the trip.

The trip meant that a huge area of my life was back to normal.

After I returned to California from my trip, I tried to determine what I had done to make it possible. I had been getting acupuncture treatments for anxiety and insomnia every week or two during the six months prior to the trip. It's possible acupuncture made the difference. However, I questioned whether acupuncture provided the improvement I needed to make the trip. In fact, I stopped the acupuncture about two months later, because I finally decided that the acupuncture–at least sometimes–caused my back to go out. Also, the acupuncture didn't have a noticeable effect on my anxiety or insomnia.

In short, I'm not able to identify what occurred that allowed me to fly to Wisconsin.

Chapter 21 ONGOING FEARS

After my "triumphant" return to Wisconsin in 1985, I was able to lead my life on a higher, more satisfactory level. In the following years I made three to five trips a year to Wisconsin, with each trip lasting 10 to 21 days. In 1990, I spent a total of 59 days in Wisconsin.

But all was not well. I continued to be bothered by my fears of Wisconsin and utilities. Mainly, I thought those fears manifested themselves in my insomnia and my continuing, but less-troubling, back problem. There were, however, other manifestations. You'll find it easier to understand my fears if I describe some of the incidents that occurred.

By May 1987, my parents were heavily into estate planning. They wanted to give their house to my sister and me. (We were the only children my parents had, and we are twins.) My parents had always given us presents, money, etc. on a fifty-fifty basis.

They wanted to put the deed to their house in our names. The idea of being owner to one half of a house in Wisconsin made me very nervous. I told them to leave my name off the deed–i.e., to give the house to my sister. And they agreed.

When was the last time you gave up a gift of half a house because it made you nervous?

In June 1987, I was in Wisconsin for a 12-day vacation. As I was packing for the return flight, my mother was folding laundry. She happened to come across the towel and wash cloth I had been using. "Here," she said, "Why don't you take these along." I put them in my suitcase.

The towel and wash cloth were new. My second day back in San Diego I threw them away. They were making me tense.

When I relocated to California, I moved my portable dishwasher with me. It was a Sears Kenmore dishwasher that I had purchased in 1964. By 1989, the machine was showing wear. I

61

thought I should get it repaired, while parts were still available, or buy a new one. I looked at a new one, but decided my machine was better than a new one, even though mine was 25 years old.

The repairman came out, and I was home to let him into my apartment. He was there two hours, and he was a talkative fellow. Mostly he talked about neutral items. Then he got into sensitive territory. "My first three years with Sears were in Indiana," he said. I wasn't too pleased to hear that.

"But where I really got moving with Sears was in Chicago," he said. "There they gave me excellent training."

He didn't know it, but that statement was like a knockout punch.

To have someone who had lived in Indiana and had been trained in Chicago come in and repair a machine would be acceptable to anyone—except me. I knew my machine and I were in trouble. That night I slept poorly.

How could I resolve this emotionally upsetting situation? I decided that if I could remove all the parts he had installed, I could keep the dishwasher. (I had the old parts, and the machine had been working. I had just wanted old parts replaced with new parts.)

I took the machine apart and reinstalled all the old parts—a 4-hour job. Dammit. The machine leaked.

I figured I could stop the leak, but I would have to use one new part. I didn't think my emotional system would accept one new part.

I didn't have a choice. I took the machine apart again and installed the one new part. The machine worked.

But I couldn't sleep.

I called the Salvation Army and had them pick up my dishwasher. It had been with me 25 years.

This 1989 incident confirmed for me what I think I already knew. My fear wasn't just of Wisconsin. My fears encompassed almost the entire Midwest. Indiana, Illinois, Minnesota, Michigan, Ohio, Nebraska, Iowa, Missouri and Kansas were all phobic for me.

In my diary, I stopped using the word fear. I called it a phobia.

In his 1986 book titled "Anxiety," Dr. Donald W. Goodwin describes a phobia as follows:

A phobia is a persistent, excessive, unreasonable fear of a specific object, activity, or situation that results in a compelling desire to avoid the dreaded object, activity, or situation. The fear is recognized by the individual as excessive and unreasonable. The avoidance behavior involves some degree of disability.

I thought my underlying fear–at the subconscious level–was that the back problem would return. I didn't know precisely the cause of my back problem, but I knew it was psychological. So it seems I generalized my fear. I had avoided the headquarters building of Wisconsin Electric, then downtown Milwaukee. I had left the state of Wisconsin. Now I recognized that my avoidance mechanism included almost all of the Midwest.

At the time of the dishwasher incident, I had not read Dr. Goodwin's book. However, I had correctly diagnosed my condition as a phobia.

Chapter 22 BUYING A CAR

In 1988, I was driving a 1976 Buick Century and looking for a better car. One night I spotted a black, 1978 Buick LeSabre on a used car lot. It was my kind of car, and it looked really clean.

The next morning I was at the lot at opening time. The 1978 Buick had only 50,000 miles on it. Soon I had a salesman at my side yakking away. While he was talking, I was checking the items I considered important. The car was a winner.

"Can we take it for a spin?"

"Sure, let's go."

When I buy a car, I don't want a lot of talk. So I always tell the salesperson not to talk, because I'm listening for car rattles and road noise–which is true. The car was so quiet they could have used it in a Sprint pin drop commercial. The ride: It rode better than a Cadillac. I was sold on it. I would have paid double the asking price.

On the way back to the car lot, the salesman asked me to pull into a service station for gas. As he was filling up, he was also talking. "Ja," he said, "I've only been working at this place a week. I'm 65 years old, spent all my life in Wisconsin, and finally decided to come to California."

That was information I did not want to hear.

I suppose I should have gone home and slept on it for a night. But I wanted that car. And I bought it. I paid $2,925 for it.

I immediately began paying the price. My tension level went up, my Valium use went up, and my feet started sweating a lot. Only my back held steady.

Once again I turned to hypnosis, the technique I had been using all along–with questionable success. I had three sessions of hypnosis, and my tension level was not subsiding.

So how long did I last? 35 days. It was something I really wanted. But even in a month's time, my tension level wouldn't drop. I drove it to a used car lot and sold it. I lost $2,500 on the car.

I couldn't understand why I was running into people from Wisconsin during these car transactions.

Chapter 23 PSYCHOTHERAPY

In June 1990, my doctor at the Kaiser Permanente HMO (Health Maintenance Organization) recommended I see a psychologist for my phobia. I didn't think much of the idea, but I agreed because there was no charge for the sessions. I saw a Kaiser psychologist for six sessions.

One of the basic dimensions of psychotherapy is the degree to which the psychotherapist interacts with the client. At the low end of the continuum of exchanges, the therapist merely restates what the client has said—mostly to convey that he or she is listening and attentive. At the high end, the therapist makes occasional interpretations of what the client has said. In my experience, there are no therapists who render frequent interpretations.

My psychologist at Kaiser was a woman, and she was at the very lowest end of the continuum. She would greet me, and then would say almost nothing at all. This is how I would describe the sessions: I talked and she listened.

Needless to say, I didn't get any benefits from the six sessions.

As I stated earlier, I didn't think psychotherapy (i.e., talk therapy) could be of any value to me. My opinion is based on psychology courses I took in college, and books I've read since then. However, my initial opinion was formed on the basis of personal experience.

When I was in high school, I fell in love with the first girl I ever dated. We dated regularly the last semester of my senior year. About a month before graduation, I announced to my parents that I was going to give her my high school ring. It was a common practice then, and it meant you were "going steady."

Well, I got quite a surprise. My whole family objected vehemently. Gosh, I wish they'd said something a little earlier, because by then I was definitely in love with her.

Lots of arguments—not much discussion—followed.

I was 18 years old at the time and I, of course, decided to stick with my girlfriend. But it was a conflict I couldn't handle.

One day, about 9 months later, I started to cry. And I knew my romance was over. It was like a slate that had been wiped clean. I didn't have any feelings for her any more. It happened really fast–in just a few days.

I moped and agonized. I tried to figure out how I could save our romance. There was nothing I could do. Finally one evening in June 1957, I talked to her and ended the relationship.

For those of you who are romantics, she entered the convent a few months later and has not left it. And I never married.

I ended the relationship, but not the chain of events. I became even more depressed. A couple months went by and I was still depressed.

Then I got worse. I started to feel like I wasn't in contact with the people and things around me. I think I can describe the condition quite well. After you drink two or three cans of beer, your sense of contact with the people around you changes. You can still communicate with those people, but your perception of them has changed. Well, I always felt like I'd had drunk two or three beers. Of course, I hadn't had anything to drink. My condition fluctuated somewhat. On a good day, I felt like I'd had only one can of beer.

Many people find that drinking a can of beer relaxes them. Some of you may think that going through life feeling like you just drank two cans of beer wouldn't be all that bad. So I want to emphasize that I am describing the sense-of-contact problem I had. I was definitely not relaxed.

Also, I want to make it clear that I was not suffering from blurred vision. I had my eyes checked twice. I had no problems reading the eye charts, and no change to my lens prescription was required.

My sense-of-contact problem scared me. I saw a doctor or two, and in short order I was put on a waiting list to receive psychotherapy.

I was on the waiting list about 3 months, and started psychotherapy in February 1958. By then I was in college and I was no longer suffering from depression. My depression ended in January 1958, the month before I started psychotherapy. (When my depression ended, it didn't taper off. It simply ended over a short period. As I recall, I was still depressed in early January 1958. But by the end of January 1958, I was no longer depressed.)

My depression lasted about a year. I didn't take any prescription drugs during that time. The depression simply went away on its own.

Although my depression ended, the feeling of not being in contact stayed.

I was in psychotherapy from February through May 1958. I discontinued psychotherapy during my summer vacation from college. I then resumed therapy when school started in September 1958. I'm not sure what the basis for ending my psychotherapy was, but my psychotherapy treatments stopped in January 1959. I still had the feeling of not being in contact, but the condition wasn't as severe any more. It wasn't until I graduated from college, in June 1961, that the feeling of not being in contact left me.

During the nine months I was in psychotherapy, I never felt that it was of any benefit. I had read that a therapist could explain relationships issues you had with your parents, but I soon decided that was a lot of hogwash.

My therapist encouraged me to discuss dreams that I had. I soon decided that was hogwash too. No one can make meaningful interpretations of dreams.

In my experience, psychologists don't make it a point to inform the client which type of psychotherapy they are practicing. I think that the psychotherapy I received in the late 1950s was a psychoanalysis-based therapy. More specifically, it was "psychoanalytically oriented psychotherapy."

I decided "talk therapy" was useless.

Chapter 24 MORE HYPNOSIS

Basically I was stuck with my phobia problem. It was an incurable illness. I couldn't think of anything else to try. By March 1993, I had gone almost three years without any activity that could have–maybe–helped my condition. I felt I should be doing something to resolve it.

In March 1993, I tried hypnosis again–with a different psychologist. He said the charge would be $80 per session, with each session to last about an hour. I think he didn't have many clients, because each session lasted about 2½ hours. I asked him to work on the core issue: Wisconsin Electric Power Co. I only saw him three times, and he had no impact on my phobia.

He did, however, help me on another matter. In August 1992, I had been hit in my face and eyeglasses with a volley ball. It hadn't been just a simple hit. Here's what happened. I was playing in the front row, and the middle man had set me. It was a poor set–high enough, but too far away from me. I rushed over to my right and dropped my arms and hands below my belt, so I'd be able to bump the ball over the net with the third hit.

The player on the other side decided the ball had broken the plane of the net, and he had the right to hit the ball. And he did–with all his might. He wasn't just an ordinary hitter. He said he had been a member of the Olympic gymnastic team from Brazil. The ball smashed into my forehead and glasses. I was lucky it hit where it did. It could easily have broken my nose. All I got was a small cut on my nose and bent eyeglasses. It was supposed to be social volleyball.

I got my eyeglasses straightened, but I found I couldn't wear them anymore. Normally, I would have just purchased another pair. But buying things didn't come easy for me.

Anyhow, after the second session with the hypnotist, I thought of those eyeglasses. I retrieved them from a dresser drawer and started wearing them again. We had not addressed the glasses issue during the hypnosis. It's my impression that successes in hypnosis are sometimes not the specific subject that is being pursued—although I can't document the basis for that impression.

I stopped the hypnosis after only three sessions, because my level of tension increased noticeably after I started seeing him.

There was a basic reason I kept pursuing hypnosis as a treatment: My first contact with hypnosis had been a huge success. When I was 29 years old, there was a 2 to 3-month period when I didn't feel well. I was feeling uncomfortable and anxious. I went to see a doctor about it. He said, "Your blood pressure is a little high, but I can't find anything else wrong with you."

I don't know why, but I decided to see a hypnotist. I looked in the yellow pages and selected one. He was not a psychologist. I had never before been hypnotized, and I took a friend along. I told my friend, "Your purpose is to control the operation. If he suggests I should pretend I'm a chicken when someone rings a bell, you interrupt the hypnosis session."

As it turned out, the hypnosis session went very well. He hypnotized me, but I didn't feel like I had lost control or become unconscious—like subjects often appear to be when they are hypnotized in stage performances. Near the end of the hypnosis, he said, "Now I'm going to give you a posthypnotic suggestion: You will have virgin thoughts about your problem in the coming days."

A couple days later, I was thinking about my "still single" status in life. At that time, almost all of the men were married by age 29. I wasn't married, and I wasn't dating anyone who looked like a prospective wife. I was concerned.

Then a slightly different thought occurred to me. "You know," I thought, "I've spent the last 10 years as single and uncommitted. And it's been quite good. If I have to live my future years like this, I certainly wouldn't have a problem with that." I decided that if I met that one woman and loved her, I'd get married. If I never met her, that would be okay too.

I recognized that this "still single" issue had been causing my anxiety. I phoned my hypnotist and told him I had resolved my problem. I cancelled the hypnosis session we had scheduled.

The fact that I resolved my problem a couple days after the hypnosis doesn't definitely mean that the hypnosis caused me to reach a solution. But I thought the hypnosis certainly could have been a factor, and I was inclined toward using hypnosis again someday.

Chapter 25 THE ACTIVATOR

One time in 1985 my back went out on a Sunday, and I decided to check if there were any chiropractors working on Sunday. I found one. He was a very good chiropractor and a workaholic. His office was open seven days a week, and on Monday through Friday he was open till 8:00 p.m. He was now my chiropractor of choice. His name was Dr. Charles.

In about 1990, Dr. Charles added a new wrinkle to my adjustments. He started using an activator. It reminded me of a spring-loaded toy gun that shoots "bullets" with a rubber suction cup attached. Only the "bullet" never leaves the activator. In my case, Dr. Charles put the activator against my cheek bone and released the spring mechanism. It would then "hammer" against my cheek bone, with a moderate force. He repeated the process three to five times. (ACTIVATOR is a registered trademark.)

I don't know how or why it worked. But its immediate effect was to make my eyes feel better. Without the activator process, my back would go out again in a day or two.

In May 1992, Dr. Charles left San Diego–much to my dismay. The office didn't close, because there were several chiropractors working at that location. I continued to be treated at that office, but the remaining chiropractors couldn't adjust my back very well. The adjustments would only hold a couple days. So I went back to my original San Diego chiropractor, Dr. William.

But that didn't work out well either. He didn't have an activator. In order to get my back successfully adjusted, I now had to see two chiropractors. First I saw Dr. William to get my back adjusted. Then I went to Dr. Charles' old office to get the activator treatment. (When I got the activator treatment, the chiropractor also adjusted my neck.) Since each office charged about $30, it was costing me $60 every time my back went out.

I asked Dr. William to buy an activator. I said I'd pay for it. It took about a month, and he had an activator. He didn't make me pay for it. Based on my experience, probably less than half of all chiropractors own an activator.

Once I suggested to Dr. William that we try skipping the activator procedure. It didn't work. I could tell I wasn't recovering properly. I went back later that same day to have the activator treatment.

Now the activator is always part of my chiropractic treatments.

Chapter 26 BUYING A HOME

In 1995, I was living in an apartment in a high crime area of "east San Diego." I had lived in the same apartment for 14 years. I desperately wanted to get out of the neighborhood and move into a home. But that was not easy for me to do. I'll explain.

In December 1982, I had purchased a one-story home in San Diego. As I was moving my belongings into my new home, I noticed that there were quite a few airplanes flying in the area. I had checked out the home thoroughly before I bought it. I hadn't noticed any planes.

Regardless, the airplanes were certainly there when I moved in. I thought there was a plane flying through every 10 - 12 minutes. That was much more noise than I could tolerate. I slept in my new home three nights. Then I moved back into my apartment.

My apartment happened to be located between two plane corridors. Airplanes were flying to the north and south of my apartment, but not over it. My apartment was fairly quiet. That was the reason I kept living there.

I rented out my San Diego house for a year, and then sold it.

After I recovered from that episode, I reviewed the situation. It took me awhile, but I determined that all of San Diego and the close-in suburbs have significant airplane activity.

I think most people would agree that there are lots of planes in San Diego. But I think they would say the noise from planes isn't that much of a problem–with the exception of Lindbergh Field, the main airport in San Diego. (According to the June 21, 2001, issue of The San Diego Union-Tribune, there are 26 airports in the County of San Diego, and this excludes military airfields.)

I decided that I needed to buy a 2-story home. The upper half would filter out airplane noise. Furthermore, the square footage of the upstairs would have to be the same as that of the downstairs. That is, the upstairs floor would have to extend across the entire home. My specifications ruled out any house with a cathedral ceiling, or one where only part of the building was two stories. Viewed in terms of noise insulation, a home that has a cathedral ceiling is basically the same as a one-story home.

It's very hard to find a house in San Diego like the one I just described.

Following is my perception of residential detached homes in San Diego. Roughly 95% of them are one-story buildings. About 5% are 2-story buildings, but frequently a cathedral ceiling is part of the design. At most, ½ of 1% are 2-story buildings like I described above—i.e., like I wanted.

In short, the home I wanted would be hard to find.

I had another stumbling block to buying a home: my phobia.

I didn't acquire my phobia in a day. It evolved and encompassed ever more items and activities. By 1995, I had a pretty good understanding of how my phobia worked. Basically my phobia prevented me from buying products (and services). If I encountered a phobic trigger—for example, a person from Wisconsin—before I actually bought an item, I wouldn't make the purchase. If I encountered the phobic trigger during or shortly after the purchase, I would dispose of the item. Usually I threw it away.

I couldn't buy any products from Wisconsin—with one exception. I was able to buy Rippin' Good cookies, baked by Ripon Foods Inc., Ripon, WI.

I had some leeway with products from other Midwest states, but frequently I couldn't use those products either.

Generally I bought products without looking at the labels. When I got home, the first thing I did was tear off the label so I couldn't see where the product had been manufactured. What I didn't know wouldn't hurt me.

In addition to the basic problem with buying products and services, I also had difficulty performing money transactions (ATM deposits, withdrawals, etc.). For example, if I made an ATM deposit and encountered a phobic trigger on the way home, I'd withdraw—in cash—the money I'd just deposited. I'd put the cash in an envelope and place it in a drawer. I wouldn't spend it.

The phobia operated on a daily basis. If I encountered a phobic trigger on Monday morning, I wouldn't buy anything the rest of that day. But I could buy something the next day. If I encountered a phobic trigger on, for example, Wednesday, it wouldn't affect an item I'd purchased the preceding day. In other words, a night's sleep cleared the slate.

One other item: The phobia didn't apply to products and services that were immediately consumed. Accordingly I could always, for example, buy a meal at a restaurant or use a taxi service.

By 1995, there was a host of items that were phobic triggers for me. Sports emblems were a problem. All lettering and logos for the Green Bay Packers, Wisconsin Badgers, Milwaukee Bucks, etc. were phobic triggers. In addition to Wisconsin teams, some other Midwest sports teams were also phobic triggers.

Vehicle license plates were a problem. Here, too, I had some leeway, but almost any license plate from a state in the Midwest was a phobic trigger.

California license plates could also be a problem. A standard California automobile license plate has a number, three letters and three more numbers. If "WI" appeared in the three letters, the plate was phobic for me. I was amazed at the number of times I saw "WI" on a California plate.

Names of people that I knew in Wisconsin were a problem— especially first names. Usually it had to be a person fairly close to me. For example, I have four nephews: Gary, David, Jody and Kevin. (Those are their actual names.) All four of the names were phobic triggers. Fortunately, the list of names was relatively small.

Reading newspapers was also problematic. I subscribed to the Los Angeles Times and The Wall Street Journal and reading newspapers is one of my main interests, like a hobby. A single word– Milwaukee, Madison, etc.–could trigger my phobia. I read the sports section only on a day that I hadn't purchased anything. I did have some leeway on reading newspapers. I could, for example, read a newspaper in the morning and buy groceries in the evening–even if I had seen a phobic word in the newspaper. Sometimes I "took a chance" and read newspapers even though I had made a purchase that day, but I would only read sections of the paper that were less likely to contain phobic words.

Finally, all utility vehicles (gas, electric, phone and water) were phobic triggers.

This isn't a complete list of my phobic triggers–even I didn't know the complete list. However, these were the major triggers.

The "rules" that I've given above for my phobia were not absolute. They didn't operate like mathematical formulas. There were exceptions and gray areas. In general, the "rules" applied 90% to 100% of the time.

I knew I would have to carry out all the essential activities involved in buying a home without encountering a single phobic incident. Obviously, the realtor couldn't be from the Midwest. The same applied to the seller. Also, the money transactions would have to be completed without a phobic incident.

In short, I thought my phobia would prevent me from buying a home, even if I managed to find one I wanted.

I set about my task of acquiring a home. I found a couple of places that came close to meeting my needs, but not close enough for me to make an offer. Then in June 1995, I found a San Diego home that looked like it met my requirements. It was located on a cul de sac and it was vacant.

As I walked up to the home, I thought, "Boy, this one looks good." I looked in through a rear window. It looked like the house was, what I call, a true 2-story home.

I had the realtor take me through the home. I thought, "This place checks out super!"

I made an offer for $240,000, subject to my living in the house for 15 days and finding the place acceptable. In other words, if I thought the home was too noisy I could walk away from the deal. (Obviously I didn't want a repeat of my 1982 home-purchasing debacle.)

The realtor suggested I make arrangements for my mortgage. Most people shop around for mortgage money. With my phobia, I didn't have that luxury. I called one bank and asked to meet about a mortgage. The woman said she could see me at 4:00 p.m.

I drove to the bank. I said I needed $130,000. "What's the rate?" I asked.

"8 per cent," she said.

I explained that if I didn't like the house after 15 days, I would be able to cancel the entire deal.

I asked if I had to pay a fee to accompany my mortgage loan application. She kind of laughed and said, "We're running a special today at the bank. You don't have to pay anything."

I drove home. I had completed my loan application without a phobic incident. I had a long way to go.

The seller accepted my offer.

My move-in date was July 15, 1995. There were lots of activities. One man was finishing roof repairs. Another man was replacing a door. A young fellow was installing new window screens. A refrigerator I had rented was delivered. Two real estate agents were there. I did the final walk-through inspection and "signed papers."

Finally at 4:00 p.m. I was alone. I then did what I considered my first essential action. The kitchen sink had an In-Sink-Erator garbage disposal unit. The word IN-SINK-ERATOR appeared in the chrome portion of the drain. I took a pan, filled it with water and placed it over IN-SINK-ERATOR. That pan would remain there for many years. (In-Sink-Erator headquarters is in Racine, WI.)

By late that evening, I had moved into my prospective home all the items I would need for the 15-day trial period. The first day had gone well.

During my second day in the house, a Sunday, there was a lot of fighter jet noise. I think they must have been holding a special training exercise that day. Even a 2-story home isn't going to keep out fighter jet noise. I wasn't a happy camper that second day.

Except for that one Sunday, I found the noise level well within my acceptable range. In fact, I thought the place was quiet.

I decided to proceed with purchasing the home, and I took a week's vacation to help me get through the home-buying process.

I had $85,000 in bonds and treasury notes at a downtown brokerage firm. The $85,000 would be most of my payment for the house. The problem was I had to pick up and deliver the money without a phobic incident. I knew I could eliminate most of the chances for a phobic incident if I used a taxi to pick up the money. But there was still a chance of seeing a Midwest license plate, sports emblem, etc. when I was at the brokerage office, or when I was getting into and out of the taxi. I thought the risks were too high.

Finally I thought of a solution. I had the brokerage firm wire the money to the escrow company. (I had never before wired money.)

On any day that involved a significant task–such as the $85,000 payment–it was imperative that I get through the day without encountering a phobic trigger. To achieve this, I tried to shut out the major sources of stimuli. That meant no newspapers, no TV, no radio and no leaving the house except for back yard activities. I also had controls in place to prevent unwanted phone calls.

In California, almost all sales of private homes are handled by an escrow company. When it came time to close escrow, I faced the same problem that I had with the $85,000. How do I get to and from the escrow company without a phobic incident?

I solved that problem by having the escrow agent and realtor come to the home being sold–i.e., the one in which I was living under the 15-day clause. Because the legal documents could contain phobic triggers, I basically didn't read any of the documents. I just signed wherever they told me to sign. (I did check the price of the home and the interest rate.)

I tried to buy the home without knowing the state in which the seller lived. Even with my limited perusal of documents, I couldn't manage that. Fortunately, the seller didn't live in the Midwest.

As of August 3, 1995, I owned the home. I think I came up with some clever ideas in order to make the purchase. Mainly I think I was just very lucky.

For those of you who are religious and think that God intervenes in specific events, I think you can use this as an example.

In the following chapters, I describe ongoing problems with my phobic condition. As you read them, you will realize how incredible the home purchase was.

Chapter 27 THE 2:00 A.M. WAKE-UP

Based on books I've read, a phobia normally involves an immediate, extreme reaction to the object or situation that is feared. For example, a person with a phobia related to bridges becomes highly agitated upon seeing a bridge, or even a picture of a bridge.

I didn't have immediate, strong reactions to a phobic trigger. My reaction would occur that night when I slept. In earlier years, I would wake up multiple times during the night when I had encountered an item that was phobic for me. (However, as I reported in earlier chapters, I used to get an immediate reaction when I made reservations to fly to Wisconsin.)

By 1995, my reaction was much more precise. If the item (or event) was phobic for me, I would wake up two hours after I went to bed. I normally went to bed about midnight. So 2:00 a.m. was the wake-up time.

If I woke up at 2:00 a.m. and was wide awake, I'd get up and throw the item(s) away.

If I woke up at 2:00 a.m. and was a little drowsy, I'd try to sleep through the night. If the item was indeed phobic for me, I'd wake again at 3:00 a.m., 3:30 a.m., and then be wide awake at 4:00 a.m. I'd finally concede the issue and throw the item(s) away.

If I made it through the night, I kept the item(s).

I'll use groceries as an example and explain why I didn't know if an item (or event) had been phobic for me. One night I bought groceries and saw a car with a Kansas license plate on the way home. I knew that Midwest states were generally phobic for me. I didn't know if Kansas was. I thought I might be able to sleep through the night, and I did.

One time I was going through a grocery check-out line, and the cashier and bagger were talking. The bagger said, "Did you hear there was a lineman electrocuted today at San Diego Gas and Electric?" I knew utilities were phobic for me. I didn't know if that sentence was. I found out at 2:00 a.m. It was, and I threw away the groceries.

These 2:00 a.m. adventures weren't always simple exercises. Usually I woke up scared. Everything I owned was at risk. Sometimes I couldn't identify the issue or phobic trigger that had caused me to wake up. And I had to resolve the matter quickly. I needed to get back to sleep so I could go to work in the morning.

If I couldn't determine the cause of my disturbance, I'd be awake again at 2:00 a.m. the next night.

In the beginning, I used to destroy the items I threw away. One time I threw away a broom. I cut it into such small pieces you could have identified it as a broom only after a thorough inspection.

During one of the 2:00 a.m. adventures, I was throwing away a broom and a brush. (I think I threw away five brooms and three brushes. So they may appear in multiple examples.) The brush was built so well I couldn't see how I could quickly destroy it. I decided to give the broom and brush to the Salvation Army, located in downtown San Diego. But this wasn't something to be done later. It had to be done now.

At 3:00 a.m. I drove to the Salvation Army location. Their parking lot is enclosed in a protective fence. I just threw the broom and brush over the fence.

I didn't like the idea of leaving the house to dispose of an item. It opened up the possibility of yet another phobic event during the disposal process. (In fact, that's why I threw away items rather than returning them.) My phobia created such horrendous tension I couldn't risk the chance of that second phobic trigger.

Also, I thought the police might not know how to interpret my tossing of items over a fence. One night I was stopped by the police about two blocks from the Salvation Army lot–after I had tossed my items over the fence. I had purchased the car a few months earlier, and there were outstanding citations against the previous owner–i.e., I wasn't pulled over for my Salvation Army activities. He let me go.

Later when I threw away items, I stopped destroying them– probably because there were so many.

One time I had a battery installed in my wristwatch, and I encountered a phobic trigger at the jewelry store. At 2:00 a.m. I was wide awake. I was going to throw away the wristwatch. God, I didn't want to do that.

Then I thought I might be able to save the wristwatch if I took out the battery–i.e., just throw away the battery. I couldn't pry open the back plate of the watch case. None of my kitchen knives was fine enough. Finally I got it open, and I threw away the battery.

Now I had to fall asleep. If I couldn't fall asleep, the wrist watch had to go too.

The next thing I heard was my alarm clock. I had fallen asleep! Oh, I was happy that morning. In fact, I was happy the whole day.

Usually my 2:00 a.m. wake-ups were related to purchases. But it didn't have to be a purchase. A few times a year I would wake up at 2:00 a.m. because there was something I should do. Those wake-ups were especially tough to resolve. Such an incident occurred in 1996. I'll describe it for you, but first I'll have to give you background information.

To limit the damage my phobia was causing, I divided my life into five categories: health, car, home, banking activities (ATM deposits, mortgage payments, etc.) and purchases not related to the preceding four categories (e.g., buying a shirt). On a given day, I would perform a significant activity for only one of the five categories. Accordingly, I could get my car repaired on a given day, but I would never buy a shirt and get my car repaired on the same day. Similarly, if I got a mortgage statement on the day I purchased any item, I wouldn't open the mortgage statement that day.

If one activity was insignificant, I could perform activities that fell in two different categories. So I could sweep the sidewalk in front of my house and get my car repaired on the same day. But if the gate to my back yard needed repairs, I couldn't repair that gate and get my car repaired on the same day.

If I had a phobic incident, I didn't want more than one major category of my life involved.

Work, of course, was another major category in my life. However, I seldom had phobic incidents at work. Accordingly, the separation of activities that I described above didn't include work. That meant, for example, I could go to work and get my car repaired on the same day.

The disadvantage of my 5-categories system was that I couldn't keep up with the processing required to lead a normal life. For example, I had mortgage statements and letters from my bank that I had left unopened for half a year.

Now back to my 1996 wake-up incident. I was awake a couple hours trying to determine what action I was supposed to take.

Finally I decided I needed to open all those unopened letters and statements from my bank. I read the letters, reviewed the statements and was then able to go back to sleep. (Incidentally, the letters indicated my bank had not received a confirmation that I had home insurance. The bank was going to buy the insurance for me and charge me a very, very high fee for it.)

During some of the 2:00 a.m. wake-ups, I tried to resist throwing away the recently-purchased item. It never worked. In the end, I always threw away the item. (Based on my experience, will power cannot overcome a phobia. You can delay your reaction to phobic pressures. But ultimately you will succumb to its requirements—because you can't stand the tension.)

When I disposed of an item, it would relax me. On weekends I would just go back to bed and fall asleep. On workdays I usually took a Valium pill before I went back to bed, because I needed to get back to sleep quickly so I would be ready for work.

Following the purchase of my home in 1995, the 2:00 a.m. wake-up became an all-too-frequent part of my life.

Chapter 28 BEING SQUEEZED

Soon after purchasing my home, it became apparent to me that I'd have to be buying a lot more than in my apartment days. Of course, buying wasn't my strong suit.

I'll describe an incident from November 1995 to show how fragile my situation was. I decided I needed a ceiling light in an upstairs bedroom, and I arranged for an electrician to do the work. Some of the work required two people, and I gave him a little help.

After he left, I wasn't feeling too well. Electricians, like many things, bothered me. The next day I removed the newly installed light fixture and threw it in the trash cart.

I still felt uneasy. I decided that in order to feel comfortable, I would have to get the new wiring removed. I phoned the electrician's office and scheduled to have him undo his work. I actually did that.

The day before he was to do the de-installation, I flip-flopped. I bought a new ceiling light fixture, installed it, and cancelled the wire-removal job. I don't know what saved me.

In early 1996, I started throwing away groceries. I briefly described such an incident in the preceding chapter. That incident involved an unusual trigger. Usually a Wisconsin symbol was the trigger.

I'll describe a typical episode. I'd have about half of the items I needed in my shopping cart. As I was putting an item in my cart, I'd glance up and see, for example, a man with a Harley-Davidson emblem on his cap. (Harley-Davidson Inc. headquarters is in Milwaukee, WI.)

Even though I saw an obvious Wisconsin symbol, my initial reaction was usually a denial. I'd think, "It's only an emblem. It's not one of my strong phobic triggers." And I'd finish my shopping.

The result was always the same. At 2:00 a.m. I'd be wide awake. I knew that meant I had to throw away all the groceries I'd just purchased. If I didn't, I wouldn't be able to sleep.

I'd take off my pajamas and put on regular clothes. (I didn't want my pajamas to touch any of the groceries.) I'd gather up all the groceries and throw them in the garbage cart. I always made sure I trashed the sales receipt and paper bags used for the groceries.

At first, I also threw away any change (paper bills and coins) I'd gotten. Later I revised that part of the procedure. I put the change in an envelope and put the envelope in a storage area.

It was doubly disappointing. Frequently I was throwing away the only food I had in the house.

In August 1996, I threw away groceries three times.

I mentioned in an earlier chapter that names of people could be phobic triggers. Jody was one of those names. Once I bought shaving products at a drug store. As I was walking out the door, I heard over the loud speaker, "Jody, to register one, please." I ended up throwing away the shaving products. For me to purchase an item, everything had to go just right.

Shortly after I arrived in San Diego in 1980, I set up an excellent arrangement for getting my car repaired. The service station I used was located less that a block from where I worked. I would drop off my car in the morning and pick it up after work. The mechanics were outstanding.

In early 1996 that all changed. I stopped in one day and saw that the interior of the shop had been completely redecorated in a Snap-On tools motif. (Snap-On Inc. headquarters is in Kenosha, WI.)

I had no choice. I had to use another shop. To get my car repaired, I started dropping it off at shops at night, using taxis, renting cars, etc. It was a nightmare.

I had considerable difficulty handling my U.S. mail. The name of a single Midwest state could trigger my phobia. That meant the addresses on letters were a problem. To overcome this, I wouldn't read my mail on a day that I had purchased an item. Of course, sometimes I purchased something two days in a row. That meant I left the mail in the mail box for two days.

I tried to coordinate my purchases with the unread mail. Four days was my maximum for leaving mail in the mail box.

From a phobic viewpoint, I always knew that my electric service bill was a problem. One time my electric bill and the title for a car I'd purchased came in the mail together. Somehow I couldn't stomach that—meaning I couldn't use the car title. I tore up the title. Then I called the Department of Motor Vehicles and asked them when they were going to send my car title. I think I called twice, and they sent me a second title.

To prevent a repeat of that incident, I rented a mail box at a mailing services store. I had my electric bills sent to my rented mail box. In terms of my phobia, that worked well.

My phobia made the handling of money difficult. During the late 1980s, I invested money in bonds. Of course, I invested only in California bonds–or at least I thought I did. In 1996, I was reading the newspaper one day and learned that one of the bond funds I owned had been created by a Chicago company. I was getting a monthly check. After that, I couldn't cash the checks anymore. I just threw them in a drawer.

I had purchased $25,000 in bonds issued by two counties in California. For many years I received interest checks issued by California banks. Then due to some buyouts and consolidations, my interest checks suddenly started coming to me from a Minneapolis bank. I did the same thing. I just threw the checks in a drawer.

I had checks coming in, but I couldn't cash them.

Nothing was off-limits to my phobia. Once I had an infection in my toe, and I saw a Kaiser Permanente nurse-practitioner. He gave me a prescription for an antibacterial ointment, and I had it filled. I encountered a phobic trigger on the way home and ended up throwing away the ointment.

When I threw away an item, I always waited a day before I tried to replace it. In this case, if I picked up the ointment on Monday, I would not have tried to replace it until Wednesday.

On Wednesday I phoned the Kaiser medical office. I said, "I had a prescription filled for an antibacterial ointment two days ago. I have a phobia, and because of my phobia I threw away the ointment. I'd like to have the prescription refilled."

What I said was probably a little hard to believe. The woman at Kaiser said, "You didn't throw away the ointment. You mean you lost it."

"No," I said, "I threw it away."

She recorded some additional information, and I got my prescription refilled.

I almost never told anyone I had a phobia. I found they didn't really understand the significance of what I had told them. They usually continued to act just as they had before I told them. In one case, the person found it humorous. (I don't have many experiences on which to base it, but I suspect the humorous reaction is fairly common.)

My job was going well. I had resolved my back problem to where it was only a minor issue. I now owned a house that was both a quiet haven and a satisfying haven. I wasn't unhappy. But carrying on the daily activities of life was getting harder and harder. I was being squeezed by my phobia.

Chapter 29 MY TEETH

My phobia was causing me lots of concerns. One particularly critical concern was my teeth. When I was a freshman in high school, a dentist pulled four of my upper, front teeth and gave me a partial plate. Over the years, three more teeth were added.

I was throwing away lots of things, and I knew my partial plate wasn't on some sacred list. I took my partial out each night at bed time. (You take partials—and full plates—out at night because it allows air to get at the gums and palate. This, in turn, keeps the tissues healthier.) When I had my 2:00 a.m. wake-ups, the first action I took was to put my partial in my mouth. I knew that if I accidentally bumped my partial with the product I was throwing out, I'd also be throwing out my partial plate.

In February 1996, my dentist moved to a new office. At his old office, each patient was seen in a private room. At the new place, the office was a huge, open area with cubicles. In other words, you could hear the drilling and conversations that were going on throughout the office. There were two dentists, two dental hygienists, two dental assistants and two receptionists in the office. In addition, they had a TV set on.

This was a perilous situation for me. Words were phobic triggers for me. My solution for phobic triggers was to throw away the item involved. That meant that if I heard a phobic word while the dentist was drilling on one of my teeth, I'd have to get that tooth pulled! If, for example, the score of a Green Bay Packers game were announced on the TV, I'd lose that tooth.

This was my solution: I got them to turn off the TV while they worked on my teeth. Also, I put tissue paper in my ears. The tissue paper wasn't 100% effective, but it cut some of the sound.

Incidentally, I wasn't willing to change dentists. I was with the same dentist for 12 years. Prior to seeing him, I'd seen two other dentists—and both of them had proved to be incompetent.

The power of a phobia is overwhelming. You are not going to overcome it. You get so tense and you want to sleep so much, you will do almost anything. On some nights I threw out products and groceries to get back to normal. Hell, I would have been capable of throwing out everything I had in the house.

I've seen on TV the pictures of parents who have a son or daughter who is missing. The strain and can't-sleep-look on their faces is easy to see. In the midst of a phobic episode, my tension was at that same level.

As I described in an earlier chapter, in 1988 I tried to keep a car that I really wanted but had been sold to me by a Wisconsin salesman. I was able to hold out about a month, and then I sold the car. If one of my teeth was involved in a phobic incident, I figure I would have held out three months. Then I would have had the tooth pulled.

Now I'll jump forward in time to an incident that occurred in the years 1998-1999. By 1998 my partial was 21 years old, and my dentist recommended I replace it. I said, "Sure, go ahead." (There had been three separate incidents where a tooth had broken off of my partial.)

He said, "I can't just replace it. I'll have to crown two or three new teeth and replace two existing crowns. I need to have firm, crowned teeth as anchors for the partial." He said it would take six visits and two months.

There was no way I could agree to such an idea. I could never get through six visits without a phobic incident—in the dentist office or after leaving his office. Also, too many of my teeth were at risk. If I encountered a phobic trigger, I'd end up having all five of the teeth pulled.

This was one of those rare instances where I told someone I had a phobia. I didn't give him a lot of details, but I did tell him I had a phobia. I told him, "If I encounter a phobic trigger in the middle of the process, I won't be able to complete it. Can't you just replace my partial?"

Even with the information about my phobia, he wouldn't budge. He maintained all the work had to be done. We were at a standoff.

In addition to the phobia issue, there one other consideration involved. I wasn't having any problems with the five teeth he wanted to crown.

The standoff continued for almost a year. I recognized that I really needed a new partial. By this time, the facing on one of my crowns was showing wear. Finally, in 1999, I suggested to him that he replace that one existing crown and my partial. He agreed.

In September 1999, I got my new partial plate.

Chapter 30 COPING TECHNIQUES

I had two main techniques to get around my phobia. One was to use a taxi. The other was to spend the day in isolation. By isolation I mean no radio, no TV, no newspapers, no books and no leaving the house except for back yard activities. I had tried both techniques prior to 1995. But the potential and effectiveness of both ideas really hit me when I was buying my home in 1995.

I particularly needed a way to visit doctors, get Valium prescriptions filled, and pick up and drop off shirts at the cleaners—and do it without encountering a phobic trigger.

The taxi was a terrific tool, because I could make trips without seeing utility vehicles, Midwest license plates, etc. I could sit in the back seat and keep my eyes closed, or glued to items inside the taxi.

I used the same taxi cab driver all the time, because he didn't talk during the trip. If he talked, he might say a word that was a phobic trigger. It reminded me of the secret word on the old Groucho Marx TV show. Only the secret word made me a loser, not a winner.

I could, of course, encounter a phobic trigger while in the doctor's office, at the cleaners, etc. But the taxi reduced the odds tremendously.

I didn't need a taxi for all doctor visits—just those where a medical procedure that was invasive would be performed. Accordingly I didn't use a taxi to see the chiropractor, but I did use a taxi to see the dentist.

I tried to do my shopping during the evening—because it was dark—and on Saturday afternoons and all day Sunday—because there were fewer utility vehicles on the streets.

My cleaners was open till 6:00 p.m. on Saturdays. During the winter months I could pick up my shirts while it was dark. The rest of the year I did my pickups during the daylight hours. And I had been singularly unsuccessful at pickups (and drop-offs).

By 1995, I figure I had trashed 20 white shirts due to my phobia. Some I trashed because of phobic events during trips to the cleaners. Others I trashed due to phobic events while I was buying new shirts. At $30 a shirt, I had thrown away $600. And my stock of shirts was down to four.

If I encountered a utility vehicle or Midwest license plate on the way to the cleaners, I stopped my trip. I'd try again the following Saturday. (Trips to the cleaners on Mondays through Fridays were out of the question.)

After I started using the taxi, my success rate went up to 100%. I felt I was accomplishing something. I was completing errands. I had suits and shoes that had been languishing in the closet. I got them cleaned and repaired.

Of course, the taxi was expensive. I was paying $1.25 for each shirt I had laundered, and $40 for the round-trip taxi ride. I once used a taxi to get my shoes repaired. The shoe repair cost $30 and the two taxi rides cost $120.

My goal was to carry out the basic activities of life—not save money.

My other technique was isolation. I used that technique when it was imperative that I complete a purchase or banking activity.

Assume I wanted to buy a tennis warm-up suit. I would normally purchase an item like that on a Saturday afternoon. On Saturday morning I'd make it a point to stay home, probably spend the morning doing some house cleaning. About 1:30 p.m. I'd go out and buy the warm-up suit. By 3:00 p.m. I'd be back with the purchase. Assuming I hadn't encountered any phobic symbol, I'd turn off the ringer on the phone and then go into my isolation mode until midnight, my normal bedtime.

The isolation mode meant I did almost nothing the rest of the day—in this warm-up suit example, a 9-hour period. My house was fairly large. I'd spend a lot of time walking in the house and back yard. The evening meal and snacks were nice interruptions. I thought it was a little bit like being in jail. Only I had a lot more room and could eat whenever I wanted.

My "isolation mode" days were really rough when an ATM deposit was involved. When my mortgage payment was due, I considered it essential that I successfully complete the ATM deposit. (My mortgage payments were automatically deducted from my bank account.)

To insure success, I would make the ATM deposit about 5:00 a.m. I didn't like being next to a money machine in the dark, but the darkness meant I probably wouldn't see a phobic trigger.

After I made my ATM deposit, I'd sleep until 10:00 a.m. Then I'd go into my isolation mode–i.e., do nothing for 14 hours. Just think about it. I would do one thing–make an ATM deposit–and then do almost nothing the rest of that day to ensure the success of that deposit. (I won't go into why I wasn't using automatic check depositing.)

The "isolation mode" days were long. But I usually felt good, because I knew I wouldn't encounter a phobic trigger and would be able to, as applicable, keep the item I'd purchased or successfully complete my ATM deposit.

Chapter 31 THOUGHT FIELD THERAPY (TFT)

In early 1997, I gave hypnosis another shot. Yes, I tried it again. I had six sessions with the hypnotist, and we weren't making any progress.

At the end of the sixth session, my hypnotist said to me in an exasperated tone, "This isn't working. I recommend that you see another doctor. His name is Dr. Bray. My secretary can give you his phone number and address." (My hypnotist also said he'd phone Dr. Bray and give him the essentials of my case.)

I was given the business card of a Dr. Robert L. Bray. His name was followed by "LCSW, PhD." I had no idea what LCSW meant. The card indicated he practiced "Thought Field Therapy." I had no idea what that meant either. (Later I learned LCSW is Licensed Clinical Social Worker.)

I phoned Dr. Bray. First we discussed his fee. We agreed on $100 an hour. Next we discussed his business location. He was located on Madison Avenue in El Cajon, a suburb of San Diego. I said I was concerned about his office address, because Madison was a phobic trigger for me. We discussed just briefly the possibility of meeting at some other location. "Well," I said, "Let's start at your office. If that doesn't work, we'll go to another place." Then we set up an appointment.

On Wednesday, July 30, 1997, I had my first session with Dr. Bray–a 1½ hour session. For you accountants, that was $150. I was a member of the Kaiser Permanente HMO. That meant I was paying the fees myself.

Dr. Bray asked if I felt comfortable in his office. I said everything seemed okay.

I started out by saying, "As you know, I have an unusual phobia. I don't want to know where you are from, and I don't want to know anything about you. I don't want to sound self-centered, but these sessions are to be discussions only about me."

In about 30 minutes I gave him my history, starting with my initial back problem and ending with my phobia problems.

I said to Dr. Bray, "I want to be able to buy products like other people."

He then instructed me on the basic procedures used in Thought Field Therapy (TFT). It was a learn-by-doing operation.

The first step is to identify an idea or words to which the client is sensitive. We used "utility vehicles." He asked me to stand up and extend my right arm straight out to the right. He said, "Think of utility vehicles and resist as I press on your arm."

He grasped my right arm at the wrist and applied about 12 pounds of pressure. My arm was weak and went down as he applied the pressure.

He said, "When your arm can't resist the pressure I apply, it means the words you're thinking are disturbing to you. That thought field is said to have perturbations. I'll treat you to remove those perturbations."

He then had me touch about eight different spots on the upper portion of my body. Each time I touched a spot per his directions, he pressed down on my still extended arm. He said, "The response of your arm—whether it's strong or weak—indicates the acupressure points on which we need to tap, and the sequence in which the points are to be tapped."

After we finished checking the eight spots, he said, "Okay, now these are the acupressure points on which we need to tap. You need to tap each point at least six times."

I followed his instructions and tapped on the points he indicated. They were on the head, hand and upper body.

Next Dr. Bray had me perform some eye movements. He had me roll my eyes 360 degrees in one direction, and then 360 degrees in the opposite direction. (In the last 20 years or so, several psychotherapies have been developed that use eye movements as part of the treatment.)

When we finished, he had me extend my right arm again. He said, "Think about utility vehicles and resist."

He applied pressure to my arm. This time it was strong. "That means the perturbations have been removed. Once the perturbations have been removed, the words or thoughts are no longer emotionally disturbing," he said.

We then followed that same routine for other words and phrases.

I arranged to see him again in two weeks.

I had two firm opinions regarding the session. The first was that I was impressed. Dr. Bray was obviously a very competent therapist, and TFT looked like it had possibilities. I wrote in my diary, "A very important day in my life."

My second opinion was cautionary. If this was a scam, I had a background that made me an easy mark. The extended arm is used by chiropractors for "muscle testing." I knew from experience that there are various chiropractic techniques that can immediately change a weak arm into one that is strong.

As I've stated in earlier chapters, I had been to acupuncturists many times. I believed that applying pressure (i.e., tapping) on various parts of the body could be beneficial.

I thought TFT was certainly good on the display level, but it might not have any substance. I wasn't quite ready to accept the idea that you could cure a neurosis by tapping various spots on the body.

My physical reaction to my first TFT treatment was not good. I needed two Valium pills to fall asleep that night. (Normally I used one 5-mg pill.) I woke up the next day (Thursday) with a cold and sore throat, and later in the day my back went out. I didn't attach much significance to the back problem, because my back was due to go out.

That evening (Thursday) my stomach started bothering me. My stomach muscles were tight, my stomach was growling, and I felt like I was going to throw up. I rarely have stomach problems, but I wasn't all that upset about it. I thought it showed that TFT had some potency.

When I awoke Friday morning, I was not in good shape. I had a cold, sore throat, back problem and stomach problem. I called in sick.

I arranged to see my chiropractor at 10:00 a.m. I paged Dr. Bray and set up a 1:00 p.m. appointment.

Dr. Bray didn't think my physical problems were related to the TFT tapping that we had done two days earlier. I disagreed.

Regardless, we proceeded to do more tapping. Using the same procedures we had used on Wednesday, we ignored my physical problems and tapped on various words and phrases that disturbed me–i.e., those with perturbations.

"Gee," I thought, "This man doesn't know how to do anything but tapping. That's his whole bag of tricks."

At the end of my second session, Dr. Bray explained that TFT was discovered and developed by Dr. Roger J. Callahan. Dr. Bray gave me a 1985 book, "Five Minute Phobia Cure," that Dr. Callahan had written. When he handed me the book, I recognized it. I had read part of the book in the late 1980s.

My stomach problem cleared up after a week.

My sleeping problems–now more troublesome after the TFT treatments–continued. I now needed two, sometimes three, Valium pills to fall asleep. On Thursday, August 14, I was awake most of the night.

The next morning I called in sick. Next I paged Dr. Bray. I waited for him to return my paging call, but no call came. I became concerned–about him. I thought, "What if he was in a car accident and has to spend a month in the hospital? I wouldn't get any treatment for months. What if he was killed?"

About four hours later he returned my paging call, and we arranged for a session that afternoon.

We did more tapping. In addition, I obtained the name of another TFT practitioner with the same qualifications that he had. Dr. Bray is a "diagnostic TFT therapist."

At the time I had gotten zero benefits from TFT. But I saw TFT as a unique treatment that held great promise for me. So I wanted the name of a backup person.

I think what I did was highly unusual. Many of you have probably been treated by a psychologist. Let's say your psychologist was a behavior therapist. Were you so impressed that you asked him or her for the name of another psychologist who practiced behavior therapy?

After my fourth session with Dr. Bray–and now two weeks after our first session–I settled down. My Valium use and general tension level returned to what was normal for me.

In late August 1997, Dr. Bray and I did a session on the purchasing of items. We concentrated on being able to purchase a broom. That evening I bought a broom.

And the following night I threw away the broom–over the Salvation Army fence.

Then in mid-September–six weeks after I started TFT–I had my first success. I had my car repaired at the service station located

97

less than a block from where I worked, the one with the Snap-On tools motif. There was nothing extraordinary involved. I simply dropped off the car late on a Thursday night. (To my surprise, I slept well that night.) I picked up the repaired car the next day.

Four days later, I took my car back to that same service station for more repairs. All went well. It was an immense improvement in my life. I drove old cars, and repairs were a regular part of my life.

Over the years the tentacles of my phobia kept encompassing more and more areas of my life. That car repair success was only the second time I'd gotten an area back. (The first time was when I became able to take vacations in Wisconsin.) I chalked up my new-found success to TFT.

I was excited. It looked like TFT could help me on my phobia problems.

Chapter 32 TFT – TOXINS

After my September 1997 car repair success, there was no follow-up act. Mostly I continued to buy products and throw them away.

Dr. Bray switched to other techniques. He said that toxins were preventing me from further achievements. TFT doesn't use the standard definition for toxin (i.e., poison). Instead, TFT considers any substance that interferes with the clearing of a perturbation to be a toxin. Under TFT theory, almost any substance can be toxic to a given individual.

To determine if an item is toxic, the person extends one arm and touches the substance with the other hand. Pressure is applied to the extended arm by the therapist. If the arm is weak, the item is toxic.

An alternative to touching the item is to simply say out loud the name of the item. For example, the person might say, "Milk."

Dr. Bray tested me and found coffee was a toxin for me. Then he found fish was toxic. Then Coke, then pizza (the sauce), then wheat. He considered wheat to be the most significant toxin for me.

I was told that if I eliminated these toxins from my diet, tapping would clear perturbations in my thought fields, and the treatments would hold.

I didn't buy it. I said, "I've been eating those foods all my life, and they're not causing any disturbances in my thoughts."

Then I said, "Your toxin theory is like the medicine man who told his patient he was sick because an evil spirit had entered his body. No one could prove there wasn't an evil spirit present. So the medicine man's thinking prevailed. Similarly I can never prove there is no wheat in my body. So you can always say that wheat, or some other toxin, is preventing the removal of perturbations."

I wasn't done. "If I removed those five items from my diet, I'd be eliminating more than half my diet. There is more pleasure in eating than in anything else we do in life. If you can't eat, you may as well be dead. In short, the cure is worse than the disease."

When Dr. Bray tested me for coffee as a toxin, the tests were inconclusive. My arm tested strong when I said, "Coffee I drink in the morning." But when I said, "Coffee I drink in the afternoon," my arm tested weak. At the time, we thought that maybe I was drinking too much coffee. This was early in my TFT experience, and I didn't know how to interpret the inconsistency.

The next session I had more information for Dr. Bray. I told him I drank Maxwell House coffee at home in the morning and Farmer Brothers coffee at work in the afternoon. I said that as a youngster I lived in a farming community, but I always said I wasn't going to be a farmer.

Dr. Bray had me say "farmer" and tested my arm. It tested weak. Then he had me say "coffee," and it tested strong. In other words, coffee was not a toxin for me.

The Farmer Brothers coffee exercise was an important learning experience for me. I learned that precise, correct wording had to be used with arm testing. Stated another way, the imagery prompted by the wording is important. I hadn't said "Farmer Brothers coffee." I had said "Coffee I drink in the afternoon." The coffee I drank in the afternoon was Farmer Brothers coffee.

Also, I learned that on important issues the same subject should be tested using different wordings–especially if the arm testing results are inconsistent.

Next Dr. Bray had me take a food supplement. Supposedly it would reduce my sensitivity to toxins, and thus make TFT more effective. I took a food supplement called MSM Ultra (Methylsufonylmethane). I tried the product for a month. It had no noticeable effect.

Then Dr. Bray had me take St. John's Worts. It's a food supplement that is said to be a treatment for minor depression. As I've stated earlier in this book, I didn't think I was depressed. But I took it for a little over a month. It also had no noticeable effect.

Dr. Bray dropped the food supplements idea.

To close this toxins subject, I'll report on an experiment we tried in February 1999. I continued to think the toxin theory was nonsense. Dr. Bray thought the toxin theory was valid. I relented and agreed to go on a no-wheat diet.

Here's what happened. On a Friday noon I started my new diet. Dr. Bray told me I should try a bread made of sea weed. I purchased a loaf. I opened the wrapper, looked at the sea weed bread, and decided I would only eat that if I were starving. I threw away the bread—one of those rare instances where I threw away a purchase without a phobic trigger being involved.

It looked like breakfast would consist of orange juice and coffee. My main meals would be jelly beans, meat, vegetables and milk.

I was committed, and on day six I was still following my no-wheat diet. Then about 11:00 p.m. my back went out. I was in bad shape. It looked like I'd have to call in sick the next day.

I thought to myself, "This is no ordinary occurrence. I've got to do something about my back." I decided I should eat some of my favorite cookies, and I did. (The cookies, of course, contained wheat.)

Within ten minutes—and I mean ten minutes—my back returned to its normal position.

I reported my experience to Dr. Bray. We never again discussed toxins.

Chapter 33 TFT – DR. ROGER J. CALLAHAN

In October 1997, Dr. Bray decided to bring Dr. Roger J. Callahan, the architect of TFT, into my case. Dr. Bray said that Dr. Callahan would not have to see me in person. Instead, Dr. Callahan could treat me over the phone using what TFT calls "Voice Technology."

I'll explain "Voice Technology" as best I can. In his book, Dr. Callahan describes Voice Technology as "proprietary . . . technology," and he doesn't provide any details. So my description here will be limited.

A typical sequence using Voice Technology would be as follows: The client dials a phone that is outfitted for Voice Technology. The therapist answers the phone. The client and therapist then briefly discuss the client's problem. In my case, I might say I have a phobia and utility vehicles trigger my phobia. The therapist then asks me to say those two words. I would say "utility vehicles" into my phone. The Voice Technology then checks my voice, and the therapist tells me what tapping I should do to clear the perturbations associated with "utility vehicles." I do the tapping. I then repeat into the phone "utility vehicles." Normally, the therapist will then report that no further tapping is required.

At this point, you can go on to the next word or phrase (i.e., thought field) that is disturbing, and repeat the above sequence of events.

The techniques used in Voice Technology are the same as those used by a diagnostic TFT therapist, with the exception that Voice Technology analyzes the voice to determine the required tapping, while the diagnostic therapist uses arm testing to determine the tapping that is needed. (In his books, Dr. Callahan does not specifically state that Voice Technology analyzes the voice. I assume that voice analysis occurs.)

I mentioned in an earlier chapter that I had read part of Dr. Callahan's book, "Five Minute Phobia Cure," in the late 1980s. I read only part of the book because I thought the idea of tapping various points on the body to cure a phobia was preposterous. So I decided not to finish the book.

I have just described Voice Technology. Essentially, a device analyzes the voice and determines what tapping should be done. (At least I hope there's a device attached to the phone at the other end.) I think it's safe to say that the idea of tapping via the Voice Technology protocol is even more preposterous.

Please, reader, don't make the mistake I made. I beg of you, read on.

Dr. Bray arranged for me to be treated by Dr. Callahan. Using a speaker phone, Dr. Bray and I phoned Dr. Callahan on October 2, 1997. First we explained my phobia problem. Dr. Callahan then had me say various words and phrases–e.g., utility vehicles, Wisconsin Electric Power Company, etc. He then had me perform various TFT tapping sequences.

I'm writing this book from the viewpoint of the consumer of psychological services. As such it includes cost figures. The cost of the October 2 session was $200 ($100 for each doctor).

My physical reaction to the Dr. Callahan session was not good. My back went out early the next morning, and it was so severe I called in sick. You may recall I also got sick after my first TFT session with Dr. Bray.

For the next several months, we left Dr. Callahan out of the picture. Then on February 13, 1998, we contacted Dr. Callahan again, using Voice Technology. Dr. Callahan had me do various TFT tapping sequences. He brought up the subject of toxins, but I wasn't willing to let him pursue that line of thinking. The session, about one hour, cost $400 ($100 for Dr. Bray and $300 for Dr. Callahan).

On February 25, 1998, we contacted Dr. Callahan once again. It was pretty much a replay of the February 13 session. The session cost $300 ($100 for Dr. Bray and $200 for Dr. Callahan).

On March 4, 1998, we had another session with Dr. Callahan. We did tapping related to my Wisconsin Electric Power Company job. The 1-hour session cost $500 ($100 for Dr. Bray and $400 for Dr. Callahan). It was an expensive activity!

My back went out the next day, just like it had the day after the October 2, 1997, session with Dr. Callahan.

I decided the Voice Technology sessions with Dr. Callahan didn't provide anything beyond what Dr. Bray was doing. So I had no further contacts with Dr. Callahan.

Chapter 34 TFT – FAILED ATTEMPTS

Our libraries are filled with psychology books written by psychologists with PhDs. Those books contain thousands of anecdotes of successfully treated clients. Typically they go something like this: Joe was suffering from depression and extreme anxiety. He reported his job was becoming overwhelming and his wife was threatening divorce. After six months of psychotherapy, Joe was able to discontinue treatment. He had regained control of his work activities, and his marriage had stabilized.

My, my, if only life and psychotherapy were that wonderful.

Just once I'd like to see a story that went like this: Mike was referred to me because of depression and insomnia problems. It was obvious he was having severe difficulties. He never missed a weekly session, but was forced to quit when his insurance would no longer pay for the treatments. After a full year of psychotherapy, that poor bastard's condition was even worse than on the day he first walked into my office.

I don't contend the psychologists' anecdotes are false. I do think they are misrepresentations, because cases of failure are normally not reported, and because many people in psychotherapy heal on their own–i.e., psychotherapy played no role in the recovery.

In line with my comments above, I'll describe two incidents I had while in TFT treatment.

On December 11, 1997, I bought a remote TV control. I woke up the next morning feeling extremely tense, and I knew it was due to the TV control. I paged Dr. Bray and within a couple hours I was in his office. He treated me to reduce my anxiety level and, hopefully, prevent me from throwing away the TV control–i.e., we did TFT tapping. It didn't work. I woke at 2:00 a.m. the next morning and threw away the TV control. Clearly it was a failure.

We didn't give up. About two months later on February 2, 1998, Dr. Bray and I had another session on the TV control. This time we wanted to do the TFT tapping before I bought the TV control.

In order for you to understand the wording we used in the session, I'll describe why I didn't have a TV control. In March 1997, I had purchased a new shirt. As I was taking the shirt out of the package, I accidentally bumped the TV control with the new shirt. The TV control fell from the table to the floor. I had encountered a phobic trigger while purchasing the shirt, and the following morning at 2:00 a.m. I was wide awake. I threw out the shirt and the TV control. (I threw out the TV control because it had been "touched" by the white shirt.)

Dr. Bray had me extend my arm and say, "White shirt and TV control." He applied pressure to my arm, and it was weak–i.e., the arm went down. That meant perturbations were present for those particular thoughts. He then determined the TFT tapping that was required, and I performed the prescribed tapping.

I then repeated, "White shirt and TV control," and Dr. Bray tested my arm. It was strong. That meant the perturbations had been removed. Dr. Bray asked where I intended to buy the TV control.

"RadioShack," I said.

He then had me say, "RadioShack and TV control." My arm tested strong. He said, "Visualize using the TV control in your home and say words to that effect."

I said, "Using the TV control in my home." My arm tested strong again.

We both concluded I should be able to buy the TV control.

I went directly from Dr. Bray's office to a nearby RadioShack store. I purchased the remote TV control without any problem. I dropped off the TV control at home, and then went back to work until my normal 6:00 p.m. quitting time. I usually took a nap after dinner, but that evening I couldn't fall asleep. I wasn't feeling well, and my heart was racing. My pulse was 104. I knew I wouldn't get through the night with that TV control. I didn't wait for my 2:00 a.m. wake-up. I threw out the TV control before I went to bed. Once again, it was definitely a failure.

My point is that even if you follow the prescribed psychotherapy practices (in this case, TFT), you may not be successful in a given incident, or even in resolving the entire case. Lots of psychology books gloss over these basic issues.

Chapter 35 TFT – ONE YEAR REVIEW

My first TFT session was on July 30, 1997. After one year, how did TFT look?

First, the negative: I've already mentioned the stomach and tension problems I had during my first two weeks of TFT. Also, my back probably went out twice due to Voice Technology sessions with Dr. Callahan.

Many of my sessions with Dr. Bray dealt with buying products. Usually the plan was for me to buy the product that same day. I would purchase the product, but in practically all cases I threw it away. Those exercises were certainly reasonable and necessary. However, they added stress and 2:00 a.m. wake-ups to my life.

Overall, the negatives were of minor significance.

Now, the positive: In September 1997, I had that one major success. I was able to get my car repaired at the service station with the Snap-On tools motif. And I continued to use that service station for my car repairs.

I feel strongly that TFT was responsible for my resolving the car repair problem. Prior to the successful repair in September 1999, I had tried twice—in July 1996 and April 1997 – to get my car repaired at the service station with the Snap-On tools motif. Each time I had felt so uncomfortable that I had gone back to the station and picked up my car before they had a chance to work on it. Those were embarrassing incidents for me.

In February 1998, I also had a success involving products I'd trashed. I'll describe the incident. Garbage pickup was once a week. If I threw an item in the garbage cart, that item was still available for one to seven days. One week I threw my new boots in the garbage cart. I hated to throw them out. They had cost me $200, and I needed shoes. On Tuesday of that same week, I also threw two new shirts in the garbage cart.

At 2:00 a.m. on Thursday of that same week, I was wide awake. I had purchased groceries on Wednesday night, but I hadn't encountered any phobic triggers. I didn't see a need to throw out the groceries. But I couldn't sleep.

I knew how strongly I felt about those boots. I had only worn them once. After lying awake nearly an hour, I got up and retrieved the boots. I put them in an upstairs bedroom. I thought that should resolve the issue, but it didn't. I continued to lie in bed awake. Finally I decided to retrieve the two white shirts from the cart. I hung them in my closet. Then I fell asleep. I had been awake from 2:00 a.m. to 5:00 a.m.

That was the first time I'd ever taken anything back from the garbage cart.

In March 1998, I started eating Kellogg's Raisin Bran cereal again. (Kellogg Co. headquarters is in Battle Creek, MI.) I had eaten the cereal for decades. But I had stopped eating it because of my phobia. It was a minor gain, but at least I'd recaptured a little lost territory.

TFT had one other significant benefit. It could lower my level of tension. A basic part of TFT is use of the Subjective Units of Distress (SUD) Scale. It's a 10-point scale, with 10 representing "intolerable discomfort" and 1 representing "total relaxation." When I went for a session with Dr. Bray, I was usually a 6 (very uncomfortable) on the scale. Dr. Bray could normally bring me down to 5 (uncomfortable) or 4 (bothersome tension).

Dr. Bray didn't treat the tension directly. He would treat the thought or phobic incident that was troubling me.

In his books, Dr. Callahan states that TFT can take an individual from a 10 rating to a 1. Furthermore, he cites two studies where, on average, TFT treatments took the clients from an 8 to a 2. In my experience, TFT usually only moved me 2 points on the SUD scale. However, I was usually satisfied with that progress.

When Dr. Callahan treated me, as described in an earlier chapter, my improvement was just 2 points on the SUD scale. One time he treated me, and I reported an improvement of 1 point. He commented, "All that tapping for just 1 point!"

The problem was that a phobic encounter would move my tension level back to a 6 (very uncomfortable).

One other item needs to be mentioned. During the year, I didn't add any new phobic triggers. It appeared that aspect of my phobia had stabilized.

In summary, I'd had three successes and hadn't acquired any new phobic triggers. But there had been no basic change in my capability to buy products and services.

Dr. Bray commented, "Today's our one year anniversary. I'm surprised you've stuck with TFT this long."

I replied, "You're the only game in town."

Chapter 36 THE BREAKTHROUGH

In August 1998, my TFT program ran out of steam. I recorded in my diary: "Dr. Bray and I discussed future strategy. We have none."

I had no sessions with Dr. Bray in September, October and November 1998. I didn't quit TFT. I was dropping out by lack of attendance.

My house is fairly large, and I often go for walks right in my house. It's an oblong path and it goes through three rooms. The scenery doesn't change, but it works. On December 1, I was taking one of those walks when I had my eureka experience. All of us have had it at one time or another. Suddenly you see the solution for a problem. It's so clear in your mind's eye you almost feel it isn't even necessary to verify that the solution is correct.

I saw that the phrase "Wisconsin Electric Power Co." was the source of my problem. I saw that I was misinterpreting the word "Wisconsin." I was correctly seeing "Wisconsin" as part of the company name, but I was incorrectly seeing "Wisconsin" as a word by itself. To resolve my back problem, I had resigned from the Company and had distanced myself from the Company. In my mind's eye, I saw that my misinterpretation had also caused me to distance myself from the state of Wisconsin. And it was "Wisconsin" as it appeared in that specific company name that was causing my phobia, my unreasonable fear of Wisconsin.

My mind was using that phrase as the definition of the issue. It correctly recognized that I should remove myself from the Company. By misinterpreting "Wisconsin" in that phrase, my mind also had me remove myself from Wisconsin.

I don't mean that I was misinterpreting the company name on a conscious level. I certainly was well aware what the phrase meant, and I also knew what the individual words meant. But in that eureka moment, I saw the misinterpretation my subconscious was making.

Of course, I don't know why I recognized the misinterpretation at that moment. After all, my brain had reviewed that company name tens of thousands of times.

I wasn't drunk. I wasn't hallucinating. I didn't have a religious experience.

I knew it was a breakthrough!

I remember when I moved to California that I knew I was being pushed. I remember thinking at the time that I could understand why a person might resign from a company. Things change and sometimes you have to leave a company. But I didn't understand why I had to leave the state.

Although I hadn't seen Dr. Bray for three months, I phoned him and set up an appointment.

On December 3, 1998, I was back in Dr. Bray's office. I was filled with anticipation. I told Dr. Bray how I wanted the company name tested—one word at a time, proceeding from right to left.

I said, "Company." Dr. Bray tested my arm strength. It was strong.

I said, "Power." Dr. Bray tested my arm strength. It was strong.

I said, "Electric." Dr. Bray tested my arm strength. It was strong.

I said, "Wisconsin." Dr. Bray tested my arm strength. It was weak! (The testing confirmed that the word "Wisconsin" in that phrase was disturbing to me.)

Dr. Bray then treated me according to TFT practices. I did the prescribed tapping. We went on to test "Wisconsin" from various other perspectives. Eventually I tested strong regardless of the context in which we used "Wisconsin."

We had previously tested the name 'Wisconsin Electric Power Co." a number of times. But we had always tested the full name, not its individual parts. According to my diary, Dr. Callahan had tested the full name the two times when his treatment, apparently, caused my back to go out. Dr. Callahan had not messed around. He had gone for the core issue.

I want to emphasize that it was "Wisconsin" in the phrase "Wisconsin Electric Power Co." that was the problem. Dr. Bray and I had tapped on "Wisconsin" in several prior sessions, but we had treated it as an isolated word—i.e., not in the connection with the phrase "Wisconsin Electric Power Co." (Dr. Bray has confirmed this recollection of our activities.)

I asked Dr. Bray if he ever had a prior case where a misinterpreted phrase was the key to solving the client's problem. He hadn't.

How did Dr. Bray feel about the session? He hardly commented. He was still promoting his damn toxin theories.

I left the session in high spirits. It couldn't have gone any better.

I expected great things to happen after that December 3 session. They didn't—at least not for awhile. I bought and threw away several items in December. Still I was feeling confident. On December 26, 1998, I bought a broom, an item I had long tried to purchase. But that night I threw it away—just like I'd thrown away all the others. Usually I threw away items and went on with my life. But that broom was different. I was deeply disappointed.

At the time it was too early for me to tell. But the door to improvement had been opened.

Chapter 37 BUYING ANOTHER CAR

In February 1999, I decided to replace the 1985 Lincoln Mark VII car that I was driving. I shopped around for cars that were about ten years old, because I could buy those cars for $2,000 to $5,000. With all the problems I had buying products, the idea of buying a car in the $15,000 to $20,000 range was out of the question. I'd lose too much money if I had to sell it a couple weeks after I bought it.

On February 15, I found a 1990 Chevrolet Euro Lumina that I liked. It had lots of miles: 131,000. But it was in good condition. I bought it for $3,300. As part of the sales contract, I had the dealer stipulate that he would buy the car back for $2,300 if I changed my mind within five days of the purchase. I thought of it as the "phobia provision."

The car dealer said I could pick up the car the next day.

At this time, I was operating at a somewhat more confident level—because of what I considered the "December breakthrough" session with Dr. Bray. I worked the next day, and then took off two hours early to pick up the car—i.e., I picked up the car during daylight hours.

Normally I picked up major purchases at night, because the chances for a phobic incident were greatly reduced. When I bought my Mark VII car, I waited until it was dark and then picked it up. I remember the salesman said to me, "I've never seen a person buy a car and pick it up at night."

I got the 1990 Lumina home without any phobic incident. However I did have problems sleeping that night. But that was understandable, since I'd had so many problems buying and selling cars. More important, I made it through the night without any strong feeling that I should get rid of the car.

Two days later I drove the car to work for the first time. It didn't go as well as I would have liked. On the way to work, I saw a

California license plate with the letters "IW"–i.e., "WI" transposed. The "IW" seemed to bother me.

I woke at 6:00 a.m. the following morning with a severe case of diarrhea. I was going to the bathroom about three times an hour. I figured in two days I'd be in a hospital.

Medicines for diarrhea usually contain the statement, "Drink plenty of clear fluids to help prevent dehydration." I finally understood the basis for that statement. After a fair number of trips to the bathroom, my so-called stools were 98% water.

Of course, I knew how to stop the diarrhea: return the car.

I also had another option: Dr. Bray. I phoned him and at 11:00 a.m. I was in his office.

In order for TFT to work, you have to be fairly specific as to the thought you want treated. In this instance, for example, I couldn't just say the word "car." I decided that one of three thoughts was causing my diarrhea:

1. Car purchase itself.
2. Mud flap with the word "Peterbilt" that I'd seen the day I picked up the Lumina. (Peterbilt is not a Midwest company, but Peterbilt has long had a strong presence in the Midwest.)
3. License plate with "IW" that I saw while driving the 1990 Lumina to work.

Dr. Bray and I checked each of the three thoughts, using arm testing. We determined that only the "IW" thought had perturbations. Dr. Bray determined the appropriate tapping for me to do. The session lasted 30 minutes.

I left Dr. Bray's office feeling a lot better. I went to the bathroom only three more times that day, and the next day my diarrhea was gone. That meant I could keep the Lumina!

This was the first time Dr. Bray and I were able to save an item I had purchased. In an earlier chapter, I described how we used TFT tapping in connection with purchases of remote TV controls, and had been unsuccessful. I thought that the December 1998 breakthrough session was the factor that allowed us to be successful with the Lumina purchase.

Clearly, the performance of TFT and Dr. Bray on this Lumina purchase was fantastic.

114

Chapter 38 CASHING MY CHECKS

In an earlier chapter, I mentioned that I was receiving interest checks for bonds I owned. However, I wasn't able to cash the checks. By early 1999, I had about 50 uncashed checks that amounted to roughly $10,000.

After the December 1998 breakthrough session, I began to feel I could take action on those uncashed checks.

On March 10, 1999, I took four checks worth $1,200 and cashed them. It was a test to see if my emotional system could handle it. I had no problems. I was somewhat lucky because the bank cashier cashed them even though they were old ("stale") checks.

On June 17, 1999, I cashed more of the checks from the Minneapolis bank. This time I was able to cash only some of the checks. The cashier and bank manager insisted that I get replacement checks for the stale checks. I kind of cringed at that requirement. Maybe the bank manager sensed my predicament, because he called Minneapolis and requested the replacement checks for me.

The next batch of checks I handled myself. I dutifully called the Minneapolis bank and requested the replacement checks. They said I'd have the checks in a few business days, and I did.

I spaced out the cashing of the checks so I wouldn't have too much cash in my home. For almost all people, money is fungible. It wasn't for me. I kept the cash from those "sensitive" checks separate. At first, I would only use the money to buy gas for my car. It was more than a year before I made general use of the money.

On a related matter, I owned a $10,000 bond that had been called. I needed to submit the bond to the Minneapolis bank to collect the money–not easy for me to do.

As I recall, I gave my phone number to the Minneapolis bank when I requested the replacement checks. The next day a woman at

115

the bank phoned me. "Are you aware you have a $10,000 bond that was called almost a year ago?" she asked.

"Yes, I know about that," I said, "I'll be sending it to you." I sometimes got into situations where my conduct was so far from normal that people I was dealing with couldn't figure out what was happening. When they talked to me, I sounded articulate.

About a month later, I submitted the $10,000 bond.

My phobia curtailed a lot of my activities, and managing money was definitely one of them.

I moved slowly. But once I got started, I was able to clear up all of these old money issues without any problems.

Chapter 39 IMPROVEMENTS IN THE NEXT YEAR

My breakthrough session was on December 3, 1998. As I mentioned in an earlier chapter, there were no improvements in that December. In fact, I threw out purchases on several different days after the December 3 session. In this chapter, I'll describe the following year–1999.

I began to get better, but progress was so slow that you can only see it by looking at my activities for a whole year.

Before I describe the progress I made, I want to provide you with a context for judging the progress a person with a phobia can be expected to make. In his 1986 book titled "Anxiety," Dr. Donald W. Goodwin states: "Phobias beginning after adolescence continue for longer periods, with about half of patients improved after five years but only about 5% symptom-free. In the older group, the phobia gradually becomes more severe in about one-third of patients."

In other words, 50% per cent of the patients will not improve and many of them are likely to get worse. A mere 5% will recover completely.

In my case, I knew I had a phobia in 1979–around the time I decided to move to California. During the next 17 years, my phobia did indeed get worse. I had only one improvement in those 17 years: the capability to take vacations in Wisconsin.

In short, it's surprising that I improved at all.

Following is a list of the improvements that occurred in 1999.

1. January 10, 1999–Encountered a phobic trigger while buying groceries, yet kept the groceries. Although I was able to keep the groceries this time, I did throw out groceries on subsequent occasions.

2. January 29, 1999–Used my car, not a taxi, to pick up a prescription. In 1999, I started using my car instead of a taxi to pick up prescriptions, shirts at the cleaners, boots in the repair shop, etc. However I only used my car about 20% of the time. Most of the time I still used a taxi.

3. February 15, 1999–Bought a 1990 Chevrolet Lumina. I described this in some detail in an earlier chapter.

4. March 6, 1999–Retrieved a boom box from my garbage cart. I had owned the boom box for a number of years. I had trashed it because I had encountered a phobic problem with a compact disc that I had purchased and played on the boom box.

5. March 10, 1999–Cashed four stale checks worth $1,200. I described this in some detail in the preceding chapter.

6. June 18, 1999–Ordered an item by phone. In the past, I didn't order products by phone. It took too long for delivery. I was concerned that if I had a phobic incident between the time I placed the order and the delivery date, I'd trash the product.

7. June 26, 1999–Had a window screen installed in my kitchen. This was significant because I had wanted the screen installed ever since I bought my house in August, 1995. It took four years because of my buying problems, not procrastination.

8. July 5, 1999 – Purchased a broom and kept it. I had also wanted to purchase a broom ever since I bought the house in 1995. I had purchased five brooms in the 1995 - 1999 period and had thrown all of them away within a day or two of the purchase date. (Straw brooms are normally held together with four rows of string. By the time I successfully purchased a broom in 1999, I had worn my old broom down to three rows of string.)

9. August 12, 1999–Started wearing my digital wristwatch again. The watch battery had gone dead in August 1998. As I described in an earlier chapter, I encountered a phobic trigger when I bought the replacement battery and threw away that battery. In 1999, I was

able to successfully purchase a battery. In other words, it took me a year to replace a wristwatch battery.

10. August 18, 1999–Left my house to pick up food, after a dental appointment earlier in the day. My dental appointments were always in the morning. After my dental visit, I would go home and spend the rest of the day in isolation (no radio, no TV, etc.), in order to avoid any phobic incident. This was the first time I made an exception to my isolation procedure. In subsequent months, I followed this new practice–i.e., isolation after seeing the dentist, except to pick up food.

11. November 6, 1999 – Purchased a remote TV control and kept it. In March 1997, I had thrown away my remote TV control. I had purchased three TV controls in the 1997 - 1999 period and had thrown away all of them within a day or two of the purchase date. I was without a remote TV control for about 2½ years, certainly a long time to be without one.

12. December 6, 1999 – Purchased a $150 camera and kept it. This was the first nonessential product I purchased in the five-year period starting in 1995.

In addition to the above improvements, there were two improvements that started in 1999, but weren't completed until the following year:

1. In December 1999, I thought I noticed that utility vehicles were no longer phobic triggers for me. One incident doesn't make a trend. But by the end of February 2000, I decided that it was indeed a fact: utility vehicles no longer affected me. I could, for example, pick up a shirt at the cleaners, pass a utility vehicle on the way home and keep the shirt. One day I filled up at a gas station while there was a utility vehicle parked right next to the gas station – something that would have been unthinkable a year earlier. This was a major advance in my efforts to overcome my phobia.

2. During 1999, I also made progress on another issue: my In-Sink-Erator garbage disposal. You may recall that when I moved into my house, the first action I took was to place a pan over part of the drain in my kitchen sink–to cover the word IN-SINK-ERATOR. On May

17, 1999, I removed the pan. The next day I put it back. On July 23, I removed the pan again. About a month later, I put it back. On February 16, 2000, I again removed the pan. Three days later I put it back. Finally, in July 2000, I removed the pan and never put it back—a 14-month project.

When you are recovering from a phobia, those impulses that once worked against you will now give you just a little help. Removal of the pan was not on my list of "things to do." Yet one day I decided that's what I should do. In at least one instance, I removed that pan at 2:00 a.m.

As you look at the list, it's easy to see that in 1999 I was able to purchase and keep several products that previously had been beyond my capacity to purchase successfully. Nevertheless, many of you probably think it's a paltry list.

I credited my progress to the December breakthrough session and ongoing TFT sessions.

Although I was showing signs of progress, I was still having way too many problems. In April 1999, I threw away groceries three times in one week. In September 1999, I threw away a non-formulary prescription that cost me $100. On October 23, 1999, I spent all the daylight hours in "isolation mode" to ensure a successful trip to the grocery store that evening. My refrigerator was empty, except for a can of evaporated milk and a jar of pickles. Keeping food in the house was still stretching the limits of my capabilities.

Note that I listed 12 successes for the 1-year period. In an earlier chapter describing my first year review of TFT, I listed three successes. The trend looked good.

Chapter 40 ANOTHER JOB RESIGNATION

On September 1, 1998, the director of my department, Information Services, announced that the County of San Diego was going to "outsource" all computer activities by September 1999. To me that meant I would probably be out of a job in one year. All of my co-workers and I were not too happy to hear the news. At the time, I had been with the County almost exactly 18 years.

During the following months, there were some changes and clarifications. In the end, this is what happened: All computer activities, except those in the Sheriff and District Attorney Departments, were outsourced. The outsourcing was effective December 13, 1999. All employees in computer-related jobs were given the option of transferring to the companies that had been awarded the outsourcing contract. In my case, I became an employee of SAIC (Science Applications International Corporation).

According to a handout I was given at the time, SAIC had more than 38,000 employees and provided systems integration, research and engineering services. From my viewpoint, I was back working for a software company. And I had lasted only three months as an employee of a software firm in 1977.

At first, there were hardly any changes. I didn't even have a change in my work location. I worked in the same cubicle and on the same projects that I had prior to the outsourcing. Only now my paycheck came from SAIC.

In February 2000, two months after the outsourcing became effective, SAIC started announcing changes in practices. I didn't like what I was seeing.

I planned on working a minimum of five more years. As long as I worked on County projects, I thought I'd be content. (The outsourcing contract provided that employees who transferred to SAIC were guaranteed two years of employment in the San Diego area.)

Then it happened. On March 18, 2000, I was going through my usual morning routine and combing my hair. I suddenly realized that my comb was almost completely filled with hair. I was suffering really heavy hair loss. I removed my hair from the comb and flushed them down the toilet.

I knew that my SAIC job was causing the hair loss. This time I was more experienced. At Wisconsin Electric, I'd gone two years without realizing my health problem was being caused by my job. I wasn't going to make the same mistake twice. I knew it was resignation time.

I didn't want to make a rash judgment. I decided I'd take 10 days to consider my job resignation idea.

During the next week and a half, my daily hair loss continued to be high—although noticeably less than on that first day.

I saw my chiropractor, dermatologist, acupuncturist and medical doctor during the next 10 days. I asked each of them for his opinion on my heavy hair loss. My chiropractor said if I was taking new medicines, it might be a reaction to them. He also said a thyroid problem could cause hair loss, but there would usually be other medical problems present. My dermatologist said my scalp looked fine. He suggested I get a physical examination. My acupuncturist said stress could do it. He said he once had a female patient that went completely bald due to a stress problem. He then added that later all of her hair grew back. "She had estrogen on her side," he commented. My medical doctor checked for a thyroid problem, but didn't find one.

On April 3, 2000, I resigned from SAIC. I had worked for SAIC approximately 4 months.

My resignation from SAIC was similar to my resignation from Wisconsin Electric. I was once again unemployed, and I didn't have any plans for my future. Just like in 1977, I was looking for an improvement in my health. I figured if I could stop my hair from falling out, the resignation would be worthwhile.

There was one other similarity. I celebrated my resignation the same way I did in 1977. When I got home, I jumped up and touched both hands to the ceiling. I was 61 years old at the time.

Chapter 41 RETIREMENT – THE FIRST 6 WEEKS

After I resigned from SAIC, I wasn't sure what I should do next. I decided that for at least a short period I would consider myself retired. I was, after all, receiving retirement payments from the County of San Diego.

In an earlier chapter, I listed 12 improvements that had occurred over a 1-year period. However, my overall status was still so-so in April 2000, the month of my resignation from SAIC. On April 11, 2000, I noted in my diary that I had very little food in the house. That meant my buying capability was still poor. Since I wasn't working, I certainly had enough time to buy groceries.

I used my new-found time to buy items. And there were lots of products that I needed. Since I didn't have to be concerned about reporting to work in the morning, I could now buy items during the week. If I had a 2:00 a.m. wake-up, I could sleep late into the morning.

One of the improvements – mentioned in an earlier chapter– was that utility vehicles were no longer phobic triggers for me. When I did shopping or ran an errand, it was usually a 20-mile round trip. There are lots of utility vehicles on San Diego streets and freeways. If I made two trips in a day, there was a 90% chance I would see a utility vehicle. In other words, utility vehicles had previously prevented me from even trying to make a purchase during daylight hours on Monday through Friday.

Now, however, I could buy items during daylight hours.

I also incorporated a new tactic into my buying practices. For more expensive items, I saw Dr. Bray before and after the purchase. I would say the name of the product, and he would perform TFT arm testing. When necessary, we did the required tapping.

Dr. Bray accommodated me in this new practice. Instead of 1-hour sessions, he saw me for five or ten minutes.

Twice I had tried to buy a new tennis racquet in prior years. And I had thrown both of them away. On April 25, I bought a new tennis racquet and kept it.

By early May, I was buying one product or service almost every day. One day I bought new tennis shoes. The following day I took in a piece of luggage for repair. On yet another day I signed up for cellphone service. I was beginning to feel comfortable about my buying capability.

It was now a year and a half since my December 1998 breakthrough session. There were now definite signs that I was making progress in overcoming my phobia. Obviously, I was recovering slowly. I didn't see any way I could speed up the pace. I couldn't ever tell if my recovery would continue.

Now let me switch to the hair loss problem, my reason for resigning. For the first month after my resignation, my hair loss continued to be noticeably high. In the following two months, there was improvement, but my hair loss was still above normal. During the next three months, my hair loss fluctuated, but I could see I was returning to my normal pattern. Finally six months after my resignation, I decided my hair loss was back to normal.

I felt I made the right decision when I resigned from SAIC.

Chapter 42 8-WEEK VACATION IN WISCONSIN

The next move in my phobia recovery effort was an 8 - week vacation (May 16 – July 10, 2000) in Wisconsin. My buying in San Diego was going fairly well. I figured that buying products in Wisconsin might be a little harder. As part of my planning, I got the names of two TFT therapists in Wisconsin.

In an earlier chapter, I described how I had thrown away a towel and wash cloth that my mother had given to me in Wisconsin. That occurred in 1987. After that incident, I never bought anything in Wisconsin that I brought back with me—with one exception. My favorite cookies are made in Wisconsin, but not distributed nationally. So each time I vacationed in Wisconsin, I always brought back with me enough of those cookies to last me till my next visit.

About a week after I arrived in Wisconsin, I made my first significant purchase: a pair of Jockey briefs. (Jockey International, Inc. headquarters is in Kenosha, WI.) I was sort of nonchalant about the purchase, because it was such a small, inexpensive item. I soon learned how wrong I was.

At 2:00 a.m. the following morning, I was wide awake. I now knew my 2:00 a.m. wake-up procedure was effective across state lines.

The next day I was treated by a TFT therapist in Wisconsin. But it didn't do any good. I woke again at 2:00 a.m. the following morning and threw away the briefs.

Four days later, I bought a pair of Calvin Klein briefs. Since they aren't a Wisconsin (or Midwest) product, I thought I might have better luck. It was not to be. I woke at 2:00 a.m. and threw them away.

The Wisconsin TFT therapist that I saw appeared to be inexperienced. So I set up a new arrangement for treatment—probably a first in the annals of TFT. I called Dr. Bray on a speakerphone. I had Dr. Bray lead the treatment, and I had my brother-in-law do the arm testing. This is the way it went.

Dr. Bray said, "Say Jockey briefs."

I said, "Jockey briefs."

My brother-in-law then applied pressure to my extended arm, and it was weak. We reported that to Dr. Bray. He, in turn, told us what actions to take next. We continued this pattern of activity until Dr. Bray felt we had completed the proper TFT treatments.

A few days later I bought another pair of briefs—the third pair. It was to no avail. Two days later I threw away that third pair.

Next I arranged to be treated using Voice Technology. (I explained that technique in an earlier chapter.) We concentrated on thought perturbations related to purchasing the briefs. The result was the same. I woke at 2:00 a.m. and threw them away—the fourth pair.

I'm not sure why, but I purchased one more pair of briefs (number 5). And, of course, I threw that one away too. It was very discouraging.

I didn't fail completely on my buying goal. I did manage to buy a pair of tennis shoes. At first, the shoes caused some insomnia problems for me. Then I got a TFT treatment using Voice Technology, and that solved the problem.

In this book I've usually described Voice Technology with three people involved—e.g., Dr. Bray, Dr. Callahan and myself. Normally only two people are involved—the TFT therapist and the client. During this vacation, only the therapist and I were involved in the Voice Technology treatments.

I played tennis on roughly half the days of my vacation. Also, I attended some get-togethers with friends and relatives. But my buying problems overshadowed the other activities.

Chapter 43 ANOTHER BREAKTHROUGH SESSION

On my third day back in San Diego after the 8-week vacation, I happened to see a car with a Wisconsin license plate as I turned into a supermarket parking lot. "Well," I thought, "I'll see if I'm any better at shopping here than I was in Wisconsin."

I got my answer at 2:00 a.m. I wasn't, and I threw out the groceries. The incident meant that I could shop and ignore minor phobic triggers. But I still couldn't overcome major phobic triggers, such as license plates.

The next day, July 14, 2000, I had another session with Dr. Bray. We did TFT tapping on Wisconsin license plates, just as we had tapped in prior sessions on Wisconsin license plates. In fact, I bet we tapped 50 different times over the years on license plates. By now, the same words, phrases, triggers, etc. kept coming up for treatment. We tapped anywhere from 10 to 50 times in separate sessions on each of the basic, problematic thoughts.

On July 25, I had another session with Dr. Bray. This one was a little different than most sessions. We spent the whole hour talking. We discussed the progress I'd made, but lamented the fact that I seemed to have plateaued. "You know," I commented, "I have so many problems. Buying is definitely the main problem. Depositing and withdrawing money is another problem. They're not even one problem. They're separate problems."

In this book, I've listed buying and banking activities as separate problems. However, until this July 25, 2000 session, I'd considered them to be a single problem: a money activities problem.

The next day, I remembered my remark to Dr. Bray. And it reminded me that, in September 1986, my parents had given me a check for $10,000. I had deposited that check in my checking account. In June 1987, nine months later, my mother gave me a wash cloth and towel. And I threw away the wash cloth and towel, presumably because of some strong feelings I had about Wisconsin. Why hadn't I thrown away the $10,000 check?

Of course, I didn't throw away the check because one just doesn't throw away $10,000. Was it possible that the $10,000 was a factor in the problems I was having with buying and financial activities? Could it be an underlying cause?

In December 1998, when I had my eureka experience, I knew I had made a breakthrough. This time I didn't have that level of confidence. But I did know I had hit on a potentially significant item.

On July 27, 2000, I was back in Dr. Bray's office. We checked out the $10,000, using TFT practices. Dr. Bray's testing showed that the $10,000 were indeed disturbing to me, and we did the tapping required to correct the condition. When the session ended, I was feeling "especially good."

Based on my experience with the 1998 breakthrough, I knew I probably wouldn't see any results from this breakthrough for over a month–although I have no idea why such a lag time should occur.

Chapter 44 A HAPPY ENDING

By August 2000, it was clear that I was capable of buying more and more products with fewer and fewer problems, especially if I used Dr. Bray as part of the buying process. So I concentrated on buying.

It had been seven years since I last bought a business suit. I had worn a suit to work every day, except on casual Fridays. So seven years was a long time to go without buying a new one. I shopped around and bought a Brooks Brothers suit for $500. In the 1996 book, "The Millionaire Next Door," the authors (T. J. Stanley and W. D. Danko) point out that most of the millionaires in their survey had never spent as much as $500 for a suit. But those millionaires never went through a buying drought like I did. In my case, I thought $500 was reasonable. Besides, I wasn't a millionaire.

I saw Dr. Bray three separate times – 10-minute sessions–as part of that suit buying process. By August 15, I was the proud owner of a new suit.

I was so pleased about it that I went out four weeks later and bought another suit.

Then I undertook a more difficult task: buying gold rimmed eyeglasses. That didn't go smoothly. I went through two 2:00 a.m. wake-ups, and I almost threw them away. But in the end, I kept them. I now own three pairs of glasses, and the gold rimmed pair is my favorite.

Because of my buying activities, I saw Dr. Bray frequently. During one 3-week period, I saw him on nine different days. A few times, I even saw him twice during the same day.

In August, I stopped using a taxi for doctor and dentist appointments–i.e., I drove myself.

Not all the pieces were falling nicely into place. In August, I threw away groceries twice.

September 2000 was a milestone month. I stopped throwing away new purchases–i.e., no more discarding of new items into the garbage cart. I think the July 27, 2000 breakthrough session regarding the $10,000 check was the factor that allowed me to reach the new milestone. (Note that over a month elapsed before I noticed results from the July 27 breakthrough session.)

For years, I took a 5-mg Valium pill each night before bed. In September, I reduced my usage to 4 milligrams of Valium each night–not a big change, but I was going in the right direction.

In October - November 2000, I took a 6-week vacation in Wisconsin. I didn't go on a shopping spree while I was there, but I made enough purchases to feel I had that area under control. I also attribute this success to the July 27, 2000 breakthrough session. (You'll recall I threw away five pairs of briefs during my previous vacation in Wisconsin.)

In late December 2000, I closed the mail box I rented for delivery of my electric service bills. I had the bills sent to my home address.

Oh, yes, I started stocking my refrigerator and kitchen cupboard with a normal food supply. I was never big on having a refrigerator overflowing with food items, but I now have it stocked at a respectable level.

In January 2001 and in accordance with what I've described above, all the outrageous acts I had been performing ended.

The year 2001 was a mop-up operation. I worked to bring more areas of my life back to normal. On the other hand, my phobic problems were not completely eliminated. And I continued to see Dr. Bray to resolve the lingering issues.

By the end of 2001, I was leading a life that was almost the same as that of most people. A notable change was that I increased my social activities. Also, I probably need to mention I started writing this book in January 2001, and that has been my main activity since then.

Now I'll give some concluding comments regarding my phobia.

For years, I had 1-hour sessions with Dr. Bray on a regular basis. Now I see him for 10 to 20-minute sessions, and they are noticeably less frequent. I think there'll be a time in the near future when I won't see him at all. I started treatment with Dr. Bray on July 30, 1997. In other words, my TFT treatments lasted over 4 years. The total cost of my TFT treatments was slightly over $16,000.

As I indicated in an earlier chapter, I paid Dr. Bray $100 for each hourly session. In December 2001, he was charging $150 per hourly session as his standard fee.

Despite all the improvements listed above, I'm not fully recovered. I consider myself to be 90% recovered. I no longer throw away purchases, but sometimes I still have a slight uneasiness when I buy a higher-priced item. I'm still concerned that I might throw it away. I tend to limit my purchases during a given day. When I'm purchasing non-grocery items, I purchase 2 or 3 significant items and quit. Finally, I still pay much more attention to where the product was manufactured than the average buyer. These are minor problems, and I think I will continue to improve in these areas.

Very few people with a severe phobia will reach a 90% recovery. I did.

James C. Schaefer

PART 2

TECHNIQUES TO RESOLVE PSYCHOLOGICAL PROBLEMS AND ISSUES

James C. Schaefer

Chapter 45 INTRODUCTION – PART 2

In the first part of this book, I described the various attempts I made to resolve my back and phobia problems. For those of you with similar problems, I think my experiences may be helpful. In this second part, I'll describe the advantages, strategies, etc. involved in the techniques I used. And, when applicable, I suggest that you use these techniques to resolve your own problems.

I believe the techniques would apply almost exclusively to adults with a neurosis, or suffering from physical problems with a psychological basis.

A neurosis is a disorder of the mind that leaves a person's contact with reality unimpaired, but results in anxiety, phobias, obsessions, compulsions or other abnormal behavior problems. Further, the disorder cannot have an obvious organic basis.

I want to emphasize that these techniques are for adults age 18 and older. I have never been married and have not had any children. I haven't had much contact with children, and, in no way, am I qualified to make suggestions regarding child psychology.

In this second part, I also present some suggestions for the field of psychology. The gist of the suggestions is that psychologists should provide patients with information as to which psychotherapies are effective for a given neurosis, and the percentage of patients who normally recover (or improve) with each therapy.

Finally, I give some comments on chiropractic treatments, Norgesic tablets, and Voice Technology.

James C. Schaefer

Chapter 46 A CHANGE IN ENVIRONMENT

One of the most successful techniques I used to resolve my back problem was the 3-week vacation. You'll recall that my back problems were more subdued during the vacation, and then flared up dramatically my first day back at work. Keep in mind that, at the time, I didn't think of my back problem as a psychological problem. I thought of it as similar to an arthritis problem—i.e., once you have it, you pretty much have to live with it.

The 3-week vacation technique has two purposes: (1) to demonstrate that you can improve (or be cured) by changing your environment and (2) to give you a clue as to the factor that is causing your psychological illness. In short, the purpose of the vacation is to get some movement, some change, in your health problem. If improvement occurs, you can reasonably suppose your illness has a psychological basis. (This 3-week vacation isn't simply some time off to recharge your batteries.)

APPLICABILITY – Following are factors to consider in deciding if the vacation technique might be of help to you.

1. Your illness should be one that is generally considered to have a psychological basis. Following are some examples: anxiety, migraines, back problems, stomach problems, insomnia, rashes, depression and bowel movement problems. This is by no means a complete list. Of course, any of the above illnesses may indeed be caused by a physical or organic problem.

There are two kinds of depression: exogenous (result of loss of job, death of a loved one, etc.) and endogenous (no obvious psychological cause). If you're depressed because you just lost a close friend, I don't think the 3-week vacation will give you any help. In short, the 3-

week vacation is more applicable to those depressions with no obvious psychological cause.

Chronic fatigue syndrome isn't usually considered to be a psychological problem. The syndrome is mentioned, but "not formally included," in the Diagnostic and Statistical Manual of Mental Disorders (DSM-IV). In my opinion, chronic fatigue syndrome is similar to the back problem I had–i.e., the body parts aren't operating properly, but there doesn't seem to be any structural damage. I suggest that persons with chronic fatigue syndrome consider this vacation technique. Just keep in mind that it's a long shot. (DSM is the "bible" used by psychologists to diagnose and classify mental illnesses.)

2. Your illness should be fairly severe. Changing your environment can involve some drastic actions–switching jobs, relocating to another city or state, divorce, etc. You probably don't want to make major changes in your life to solve minor illnesses.

3. Your illness should be relatively new–i.e., less than two years. If you've had your problem for 10 years, and you've changed jobs and got a divorce during that 10-year period, the chance of success with a 3-week vacation is probably quite low. However, if you've led a stable life during the 10 years (same job, same spouse, etc.), you may want to give the 3-week vacation a try.

4. If you've had two consecutive illnesses that are usually considered to have a psychological basis, you may want to try the 3-week vacation. In my case, first I had a back problem; then I was plagued by sleeping problems. The second illness occurred because there was ongoing stress in my environment.

5. If you have pressures that you can't escape (example: money problems), a 3-week vacation probably isn't going to help.

6. The 3-week vacation is to be used when there are unknowns. If you don't know if your illness is psychological, or if you don't know what is causing your often psychologically-based illness, then use the

vacation technique. If you know your insomnia is due to work pressures, you have no need for this technique.

ARRANGEMENTS – Following are factors to consider in arranging your vacation.

1. Try to take the vacation alone. If something in your environment is causing your problem, you want to make a 100% break from your normal activities. So you want to separate yourself from your spouse, children, job, etc. For example, visit your sister in another state. In line with this thinking, don't plan on checking your e-mail at work.

2. Try to structure the vacation so that if you improve, you'll have some idea as to what is causing your illness. Keep in mind that if your health improves, you still have to determine the cause of your illness. If you think your in-laws are causing your constant headaches, take a vacation where you avoid all contact with your in-laws.

Usually, you'll arrange your vacation so there is some balance between the objective of improving your health, and the objective of finding the activity (or condition) that is creating the health problem.

3. Be sure to schedule doctor appointments, if you think it would be advantageous for your health to be monitored during the vacation.

4. Consider taking a vacation that is longer than 3 weeks. Incidentally, I'm not too keen on 2-week vacations. I don't think it's long enough for your body and mind to react to the new environment. If your health improves the last two days of a 2-week vacation, have you had enough improvement to justify making major changes in your life?

ALTERNATIVES – Following are some alternatives to the 3-week vacation technique.

1. Consider whether you've already taken the equivalent of the 3-week vacation. Maybe you live in New York and your company had you on a 3-week special project in Chicago. How did you feel during those 3 weeks? Let's assume that you have stomach problems. Did

you for some strange reason eat pizza–a food you normally avoid–while you were in Chicago? If so, that would suggest that a change of environment might help your health problem.

Keep in mind that you need to make an almost 100% break from your current environment. If you phoned your home office and your spouse regularly during the 3 weeks, you didn't take the equivalent of the 3-week vacation I'm suggesting.

2.   Send your in-laws, assuming they live with you, on a 3-week vacation, and you stay home.

3.   Make substantial changes in your normal living pattern. If you're working two jobs, try working only one job for 3 weeks. If your illness seems to be worse on weekends, set up completely different activities on weekends.

EVALUATION – Following are considerations for evaluating the results of your 3-week vacation.

1.   Factor into your thinking the fact that most people feel just a little more relaxed when they are on vacation. If your illness improves 5% on your vacation, that's probably not enough. The improvement should be in the 20% and higher range, particularly toward the end of the vacation. Don't expect a cure during your vacation. What you're hoping for is enough improvement so that you'll recognize your illness is one that will improve (or be cured) by changing your environment.

2.   Pay special attention to your mental and physical reactions when you return from your vacation. That's a key part of the experiment – and you are running an experiment. Does your illness flare up? If the illness showed no changes during and after the vacation, there's a good chance it's not a psychological illness. The other possibility is the vacation wasn't structured properly–i.e., the factors causing the psychological illness were present throughout the vacation.

3. Recognize that your illness might not be psychological. If you have an undiagnosed cancer, you're probably not going to improve during the vacation. You may even get worse.

SUMMARY – Following are summary comments.

1. Many people are not in a position to take a 3-week vacation such as I described. Recognize that you are in a high-stakes situation. If you have a serious psychological illness, you may end up not being able to work at all. So pursue a solution aggressively. Consider taking a leave of absence. If necessary, borrow money.

2. Recognize that you may have to incur a major loss to change your environment. When I resigned from Wisconsin Electric, I knew I could never get a job as good as the one I had. And I never did. (However, I want to note that my work at the County of San Diego was quite satisfying.)

3. If you choose to make extensive changes in your environment, be sure you don't burn your bridges. You never know if subsequent events will make it necessary to undo those changes.

4. The basic concept behind this technique is that your mind and body respond to your environment, and fairly quickly. If your current environment is causing psychological illnesses, you can detect that fact by removing yourself from that environment for a short period.

5. People have many different psychological illnesses. No one technique is going to expose all psychological illnesses. Use your best judgment as to whether a 3-week vacation might work for you.

Chapter 47 WORDS AND PICTURES AND YOUR NEUROSIS

The key to my case was my eureka experience involving the phrase, "Wisconsin Electric Power Company." I don't think I'm unique. That means there are other people with neuroses that also have words and phrases in their minds that are preventing them from healing.

I think it isn't just words and phrases that can be the problem. It could easily be a picture. It's anything in the mind's eye. So it could be anything perceived by the five senses and stored in the mind—i.e., picture, sound, smell, taste or physical sensation. From a practical viewpoint, I think words and pictures will cover 99.9% of the cases.

So who is likely to be suffering from misinterpreted words and pictures? It's very hard to tell. I think the most likely candidates are people who meet the following three conditions: They are performing actions that are completely contrary to their own best interest, they know the actions are contrary to their interests, and the actions are beyond their control. I'll use myself as an example. When I threw out groceries, that was completely contrary to my best interest, and I certainly knew it. And, basically, those actions were beyond my control.

The behavior that is contrary to your desires must be persistent. If your actions seem a little bizarre, but they only occur a couple times, you're not a candidate.

People who are addicted to alcohol, drugs, etc. are probably not candidates—even though they would meet the above description. It doesn't seem reasonable to think that alcoholics are suffering from misinterpreted words and pictures. If they were, the Alcoholics Anonymous program wouldn't work.

Similarly, people with compulsions, such as hand washing, are probably not candidates. It doesn't seem reasonable, for example, that ten people have a misinterpreted word, and they all end up performing compulsive hand washing as a result of their misinterpretations. I would think that each person would perform some unique, but unwanted, action.

In short, persons who are performing actions that are contrary to their own desires when involved in the ordinary activities of life – driving a car, shopping, dining at a restaurant, etc.–are the most likely candidates.

Also, I think people who are upset by a single, ordinary item may be good candidates. For example, if you find that fans upset you, you're a candidate. (However, I don't think you are a candidate if you're upset by an item that almost all people fear–e.g., snakes, mice, etc.).

How do you find this misinterpreted word or picture? It's harder than finding the proverbial needle in a haystack. The misinterpreted word came to me in a eureka experience, but only after 20 years!

Here are my suggestions.

1.   Simply recognize that this phenomenon exits. It may make your mind conducive to presenting the misinterpreted data to you.

2.   I successfully identified the misinterpreted word–i.e., Wisconsin. Check to see if there are any elements in my case that might apply to your case. It doesn't have to be a company name. It could be a company slogan, an in-house cliché, your work address, etc.

3.   In many cases of neurosis, there is a precipitating event. Look for the misinterpreted word or picture somewhere in that event. If you were involved in a car accident, and now you have a fear of bridges, look for something that occurred just before the accident that suggests bridges.

4.   Look for major items or events. If you have a phobia about driving, it's not because some kid threw a water balloon at your car. It's because someone threw a rock into your windshield from an overpass.

5.   Look at events that occurred around the time your illness started. There is no need to look at events that occurred in your childhood. (In

the book, "Breakdown," psychologist N. S. Sutherland states that there is little evidence to support the contention that events in early childhood predispose an individual to mental illness.)

6.   Try word associations. If your illness started with a car accident, what do you associate with "accident," "car," "hospital," and similar words? There are several ways you can do this word association: paper and pencil, in your mind, etc.

7.   Be receptive to seeing the misinterpretation just before you drop off to sleep, in the middle of the night, or just as you are waking. I saw my misinterpretation while I was walking, but I think sleeping times are when eureka experiences are common. If a clarification of a misinterpretation comes to you in the middle of the night, write it down immediately so there's no chance you'll forget it.

Keep in mind that you may not get the actual clarification. You may get a phrase that leads you to the clarification. For example, let's say the name Claudia Smith comes to you. What do you associate with her? Assume it's a new, yellow Ford Escort car. You may then remember that when you were in your car accident, you were thrown and landed next to a yellow Escort car, and it had a bumper sticker with a message that's been haunting you.

8.   Try self-suggestion. Just before going to sleep for the night, lie on your bed in a relaxed position. Close your eyes and say to yourself: "I have a word or a picture in my mind that is causing my illness. When I wake in the morning, I would like that word or picture presented to me." Repeat that wording to yourself 5 to 10 times.

A variation of this would be to see a hypnotist. Ask the hypnotist to give you a posthypnotic suggestion that the word or picture causing your illness should be presented to your conscious mind.

9.   Try the self-suggestions (See item 8 above.) for 3 or 4 weeks. If it doesn't work, I suggest you drop the subject—at least for awhile. You may want to try again, in a couple months. When your mind is ready, it will present the data to you. My one case doesn't prove that this is a wide-spread phenomenon. So it's possible you're trying to find something that doesn't exist.

Once you discover the misinterpreted word or picture, you're well on your way to recovery. In a eureka experience, you know you've found the answer. I think that normally just understanding the misinterpretation should be sufficient—i.e., no further action should be required. However, it's highly probable that perturbations are present for the thought. Accordingly, I suggest you see a TFT therapist.

It's possible that some of you may already have gone through the eureka experience of locating the misinterpreted word or picture, yet your condition has not improved. In that case, rush right over to your nearest TFT therapist.

Once the misinterpreted word was found in my case, I started to recover—although slowly.

Psychology books often state that the client needs to change his or her attitude in order to recover. Frequently, it is stated that the person has to change his or her perception of events. Those concepts probably are valid for many cases, but they didn't apply to mine. I didn't change my attitude or any perceptions of events.

The chances of finding a misinterpreted word or picture are very slim. But the payoff for finding that misinterpretation could be huge: the resolution of your neurosis.

I'm sure my experience can be duplicated by others, but not nearly enough of them.

Chapter 48 PSYCHOTHERAPY – SUCCESS AND FAILURE RATES

Psychoanalysis was ushered into the world in 1900 with Freud's book, "Interpretation of Dreams." That means psychologists have been practicing talk therapy for over 100 years, but we still don't know if it is effective.

To my knowledge, no definitive study that is acceptable to the scientific community has confirmed the effectiveness of psychotherapy. In other words, there has never been an acceptable study that compared an "experimental group" against a "control group." That, of course, is the standard scientific method used to validate new drugs and medical procedures.

Although there has been no definitive study, there have been hundreds–probably thousands–of studies of psychotherapy. They vary greatly in scientific quality. Following are the findings of some of those studies.

Patients that are given psychotherapy will improve or recover about two-thirds of the time. That statistic has remained basically constant for roughly the last 50 years, and there are a number of studies to confirm that statistic.

My college textbook, "The Psychology of Adjustment," reported on a study that was made to compare two types of psychotherapy. One group of 25 clients was given analytically-oriented psychotherapy, and another group of 25 clients was given client-centered psychotherapy. The study determined that both methods of treatment resulted in 17 clients that improved and 8 who were unimproved. That is, 68 per cent improved and 32 per cent did not. ("The Psychology of Adjustment" was authored by Laurance F. Shaffer and Edward J. Shoben, Jr.)

The authors of my college textbook then state: "The conclusion seems well established that psychotherapy, as practiced by adherents of several different schools of theory, is evaluated as successful about two-thirds of the time."

In a 1993 book titled "What You Can Change & What You Can't," the author Martin Seligman provides recovery percentages for panic attacks, phobias, obsessive-compulsive disorders and depressions. The average recovery rate for the four categories is 72%.

The November 1995 issue of Consumer Reports states in an article on psychotherapy, "Among people no longer in treatment, two-thirds said they'd left because their problems had been resolved or were easier to deal with." The remark was based on information supplied by 4,000 readers. Although Consumer Reports isn't normally quoted in psychological studies, this survey was accepted as meeting scientific standards. One finding of the survey is mentioned in the textbook, "Abnormal Psychology and Modern Life" (Carson et al., 2000).

Even if patients don't get psychotherapy, about two-thirds will recover. However, there aren't as many studies to confirm that statistic. On this particular subject, the authors of my college textbook state: "Of psychoneurotic patients admitted to mental hospitals in the United States, 66 per cent are discharged as recovered or improved within one year ... Few if any of them received formal psychotherapy."

In the 1976 book, "Breakdown," psychologist N. S. Sutherland states: "Most neurotics recover in the course of time whether or not they are treated ... Between a half and two thirds are either better or much improved within two years of the onset of their illness."

I should point out that some studies have shown that untreated patients do not fare as well as those who receive psychotherapy. In the 1993 book by Morton Hunt, "The Story of Psychology," a study by the National Institute of Mental Health is quoted: "Patients treated by psychosocial therapies show significantly more improvement in thought, mood, personality, and behavior than do comparable samples of untreated patients." Since no statistics were provided, it's hard to say how noteworthy the study was.

Further, the 1993 book by Morton Hunt cites a meta-analysis of 475 studies that compared the results for patients who received psychotherapy with untreated persons. The conclusion was:

> Psychotherapy benefits people of all ages ... The
> average person who receives therapy is better off at
> the end of it than 80% of the persons who do not. This
> does not, however, mean that everyone who receives
> psychotherapy improves. The evidence suggests that
> some people do not improve ...

(Mr. Hunt attributes the quote to "The Benefits of Psychotherapy" by
M. L. Smith, G. V. Glass and T. L. Miller.)

The above statement certainly supports the effectiveness of
psychotherapy. However, it's hard to analyze the statement. Did two-
thirds of the treated patients recover? What per cent of the untreated
persons recovered?

In the above paragraphs, I've discussed the two-thirds who
recover. Following are some remarks regarding the one-third who
don't recover.

I personally have seen five different "talk therapists" over the
years, and not one gave me the feeling he or she was in control and
could resolve my case. Here's what I found: (1) Although they
appeared to be experienced psychotherapists, they gave me the
feeling that I was only about the second patient they'd seen–i.e., they
were learning right along with me. (2) They are never able to use a
prior experience to resolve an issue. For example, they'll never say
they had another patient with a similar problem, and that patient
resolved the problem by switching professions. (3) There is no plan.
Not only is there is no written plan, I got the impression there was
no plan in the back of their minds either. About the only plan seemed
to be that we would be talking. (4) There was no time schedule. If you
break your leg, the doctor might say it will take six to eight weeks to
heal. If you have a phobia about rabbits, don't expect your talk
therapist to say it will take about four to six months to cure. He or
she doesn't have a clue.

In his 1976 book, psychologist N. S. Sutherland describes how
he had a mental breakdown and searched for help from
psychotherapists, drugs, etc. He takes his own profession to task. He
states: "Unfortunately, existing forms of psychotherapy have little
effect on recovery."

He also states: "The therapist . . . by making encouraging
noises, may try to alleviate the patient's current distress."

Finally, Sutherland says: "It is not obvious how psychotherapy is supposed to effect . . . cures."

In his 2001 book, "Tapping the Healer Within," psychologist Dr. Roger J. Callahan says:

> But I felt strongly that, as a profession, modern psychotherapy was letting patients down ... They simply weren't being helped ... Some of my fellow psychologists and I often discussed our dismal track record ... We agreed that only a small percentage of our patients ever got better.

Because the fundamental issue of whether psychotherapy is effective has never been clearly resolved, the field appears to have trouble moving to other issues. For example, no well-known studies have addressed the next question to be resolved: Why don't one-third of the patients recover?

It seems to me that the one-third is more important than the two-thirds who recover—with or without treatment. After all, I was part of that one-third group for many years.

Have you ever read a psychology book that was devoted to discussing the one-third of neurotic patients that don't recover?

If you're sick, you feel you need to take action to resolve your illness. So you look around and latch onto some treatment that you think might help. One of the benefits of psychotherapy is that it makes you feel like you're doing something for your illness, even if the treatment might not actually be helping you.

In general, psychology books do not provide statistics on psychotherapy's success (or failure) rate. I searched a lot of books to find the statistics presented here.

In summary, about two-thirds of persons with a neurosis will improve (or recover). Furthermore, it appears that the average person who receives psychotherapy will be "better off" than an untreated person.

Chapter 49 WHICH PSYCHOTHERAPY WORKS BEST

In the 1993 book, "The Story of Psychology," Morton Hunt states, "All forms of [psycho]therapy appeared to benefit about two thirds of the patients." In other words, we don't know which type of psychotherapy works best, and we don't know which psychotherapy is best for a given illness.

Is psychoanalysis the most effective therapy for obsessive-compulsive disorders? Are some psychotherapies simply useless? The questions can't be answered because statistics on the results of psychotherapy are woefully inadequate.

The client pays $50 to $500 an hour for a psychotherapist's services. In a significant percentage of cases, those services may have a value of zero. The problem is we have no idea which type of psychotherapist provides a service of value and which one provides a service with no value.

By now, there should be simple charts available to direct the patient to the appropriate therapy. Each chart should show the name of the neurosis, the type of psychotherapy most effective for that neurosis, the recovery rate, the relapse rate and the number of treatments (sessions) normally required. The chart should list recommended prescription drugs, plus remarks about side effects.

The 1993 book, "What You Can Change & What You Can't," by Martin Seligman contains charts similar to what I just described. He has made a good start, but more data is needed. His charts are spread throughout the book. The charts need to be available in a single book or manual.

Although I've included a couple of quotes in this book indicating all psychotherapies are equally effective, there are indications that psychologists are finding some therapies to be better than others. In the 1993 book, Morton Hunt states:

> Some therapies are more effective than others in treating particular disorders ... the superiority of behavior and cognitive-behavior therapies for panic attacks and other anxiety disorders; of cognitive therapy for social phobias; of group therapy for personality disorders; and of both cognitive-behavior and interpersonal therapies . . . for depression.

In his 1993 book, Martin Seligman states, "Psychoanalysis does not work on phobias." Knowing which therapy does not work is certainly useful information.

In this book, I've documented how I wandered from one psychotherapist to another trying to find a cure. Because of my experience with psychotherapy while I was in college, I knew "talk therapy" wouldn't be of any help to me. So my wandering was confined to "non-talk therapies" (TFT and hypnotherapy). I was a fairly typical neurosis client. I think it's safe to say there are tens of thousands of clients with neuroses wandering about as I did. One reason we go through this search is because insufficient data on psychotherapies is available.

If detailed information that I've described above were compiled and made available to patients, doctors and psychologists, the relatively low success rate of "about two-thirds" for psychotherapy could be raised. And clients would do a lot less wandering from therapist to therapist.

Chapter 50 WHAT TO DO

If you have a neurosis (depression, phobia, etc.) or a physical illness that may have a psychological cause, what should you do? Based on my experience, here are some suggestions.

1. Physical problems – See a medical doctor to rule out that your illness doesn't have a physical basis. You probably should see a second medical doctor–to get a confirming opinion.

2. Your environment – Review your environment, looking for anything that might be upsetting you. In particular, look for any changes that occurred around the time your illness started. If major changes occurred at your job, maybe you need to switch employers.

In this book, I've tended to suggest making major changes to your environment–i.e., relocation, job change, etc. Consider making moderate changes to your environment. Here are some examples. If you're a computer programmer working on accounting systems, try switching to non-accounting systems. If you are having job problems, consider transferring to a different department. If you're a landlord and you have an apartment building that keeps giving you headaches, sell it and get another one in a different part of town.

3. Discussions – Discuss your problem with a friend, family member, priest, minister, etc. Usually a discussion with one person isn't enough. Plan on talking to several of them. Pick your advisors carefully. After all, you don't want everyone and his brother to know about your problem. Maybe just talking about the problem will help. An outside opinion, or one with a different viewpoint, may be of value. Probably the main advantage of the discussions is that by verbalizing the problem you will see a solution. The solution may even come to you as you're describing the problem.

Some of the psychologists who are critical of psychotherapy have suggested you use, for example, a friend instead of a psychotherapist. Meet with him or her on a regular basis to discuss your problem.

If you're younger (under age 35), talk to at least one person who is a generation older than you. Older people have "experiences of life" to help them give advice.

4.   Goals in life – Determine if your current activities are consistent with your goals in life. If your goal in life is to teach, will your current job lead to some type of teaching job? Is the goal you selected really the right goal for you? Are you majoring in teacher education because you want to be a teacher, or because your mother was a teacher? What is your gut feeling about the issue? I think the goals issue is particularly important for persons in the ages 18 to 21. If you've just started college and are having health problems, look at whether you have the right major and are at the right college. If you have diarrhea and you think it has a psychological basis, you're in the wrong environment–i.e., the wrong job, the wrong school, the wrong love relationship, etc.

5.   Three-week vacation – I described the 3-week vacation technique in an earlier chapter.

6.   Psychotherapy - Hypnosis – I tried hypnosis (hypnotherapy) for months and months, mainly because I didn't think there was any alternative. Except for one success, it wasn't effective. If you try hypnosis, I suggest you do it only for a limited period. If you don't get any improvement after six sessions, discontinue it. If you're not successful with one hypnotist, you may want to try a second one. I am referring here to using hypnosis for a neurosis. I am not referring to use of hypnosis to stop smoking, lose weight, etc.

7.   Psychotherapy - TFT – Of course, I consider TFT to be the best therapy available and highly recommend it. In the following chapter, I give further information regarding my recommendation.

8.   Psychotherapy - All other types – There are many other psychotherapies, substantially more than 100. As I indicated in an

earlier chapter, some studies indicate they all have a success rate of about 67%.

In selecting a psychotherapy, I think you can beat the 67% rate if you make the correct choice between "talk therapies" and "non-talk therapies." In "talk therapies," discussions between the patient and the therapist are expected to produce a cure. The prime examples are psychoanalysis-based therapies. Another example is humanistic therapy.

In "non-talk therapies," activities outside of discussions are the means to a cure. In TFT, "tapping" is the basic technique. In hypnotherapy, the hypnotist uses suggestions as the main method. In desensitization therapy by behaviorists, exercises involving the feared object or activity are performed.

Select between the two major categories according to your personality and the type of neurosis you have. If you expect that prescription drugs will be required for your treatment, you may have to choose a therapy practiced by a psychiatrist, since they are the only psychotherapists who can write prescriptions. Of course, sometimes the primary care physician can write those prescriptions for you. (There is at least one exception to the statement that only psychiatrists can write prescriptions. In March 2002, New Mexico passed a law allowing psychologists who have undergone the appropriate training to prescribe psychotropic drugs.)

9. Relaxation methods – Relaxation methods such as meditation, biofeedback, etc. may have some benefit for minor irritations. However, if you have a major issue that is bothering you, those methods won't work. You have to solve the specific issue that is bothering you.

For example: The radios at work irritated me and made me tense. I knew how to do meditation, but I knew that wouldn't be of any help. Radios were the issue. I had to get those radios turned off, or move to a place where I couldn't hear them.

Of course, many times you don't know what is bothering you. So you don't know what you have to correct, move away from, or move to.

In the October 10, 2001 issue of the Journal of Clinical Psychology, Dr. Callahan states, "I used to teach Progressive Relaxation to clients ... I found when the clients had severe psychological problems it was simply impossible to teach them to relax."

10. Coping techniques – To cope with my phobia, one of the most significant techniques I used was the taxi cab. It gave me a way around the phobic triggers. If you have a serious neurosis, at some point, you will admit there are some activities you are simply incapable of doing. Try to think of a way that you can continue to perform those activities by using techniques that are outside the normal practices.

11. Diary – Keep a diary. Psychological illnesses last a long time. Your diary will help you to spot trends. It will be your record of what works and what doesn't work for you. You'll see lots of doctors. In your diary, record the doctor's name and also his or her specialty. (I use the term "diary." You may prefer to call it a daily journal.)

You may recall that in my July 2000 breakthrough session, Dr. Bray and I discussed a $10,000 bank deposit. That $10,000 deposit was made in 1986–fourteen years earlier. I used my diary to verify what happened and when it occurred. I then used that information for the TFT treatment. (Fourteen years is a long way to go back, but it was a 20-plus-years problem.)

12. Misinterpreted words and pictures – I listed in an earlier chapter my suggestions to get misinterpreted words and pictures presented to your conscious mind.

13. Gut feelings and hunches – Be aware of your gut feelings and hunches. Follow your gut feelings in making decisions to resolve your problems. When you have psychological illnesses, you need to be aware of subtle feelings in order to reach a solution.

Avoid spur-of-the-moment decisions. If your gut feeling is to pursue a certain action and the situation permits it, sleep on it for a night. Then verify the next day that your gut feeling is still the same.

When the situation calls for an immediate decision, follow your hunches.

14. Prescription drugs – I was pretty conservative on using drugs to help me. I used Valium, but it's a mild tranquilizer and my dosage was very small. Psychological illnesses can be pretty devastating. So I think it's reasonable to try some prescription drugs for help. Rely on your own judgment–not the doctor's–as to when the side effects are too severe. If you take prescription drugs and you find the "cure" is worse than the disease, stop taking them.

If you've been taking significant dosages of psychotropic drugs for several years, try to discontinue use of the drugs. Try some of the techniques that I suggested above. Because the drugs mask underlying problems, I think it's safe to say that eventually you'll get even sicker.

15. Passage of time – Many psychological problems resolve themselves over time. I think that taking action "early on" to resolve your neurosis (or physical illness with a psychological cause) is always the best approach. However, keep in mind that the passage of time itself may alleviate your condition. Usually you can allow 6 months to a year as a self-healing period. After that, you need to take aggressive action to resolve your problem. The nature and severity of the illness will almost dictate the speed at which you will act.

The depression I had when I was 18 (described in an earlier chapter) is an example of a psychological problem that was resolved with the passage of time.

16. Managing your own case – I think psychological problems require the individual to take an active role in resolving his or her case. Based on my experience, a psychotherapist will listen to you describe your thoughts and feelings, but he or she won't give you much in the way of specific advice as to changes you should make in your actions or life style. You need to make those decisions on your own.

Psychological problems are very difficult to identify and resolve. In my case, it was a 20-plus-years process.

Chapter 51 TFT – THE THERAPY I RECOMMEND

It won't come as any surprise when I say that I think TFT is by far the best psychotherapy available. But I need to add that I was only one case, and one case doesn't prove the effectiveness of a therapy. Also, TFT would not have solved my case without my contribution from the eureka experience. (On the other hand, I couldn't have recovered without TFT–i.e., I needed both the eureka experience and TFT.)

TFT suffers from the same problem as all psychotherapies. There are no statistics available from unbiased sources as to its effectiveness. In short, I do not have any statistics to back up my recommendation. Furthermore, I don't even have an anecdote of a TFT patient who I personally know was successfully treated by a TFT therapist.

But I do have years of experience with TFT treatments, as documented in this book. Also, I have experience with non-TFT therapies. And on the basis of those experiences, I recommend TFT as the first psychotherapy to try.

Dr. Roger J. Callahan, the architect of TFT, has written three books about TFT. You may find them of interest.

1. Five Minute Phobia Cure (1985)
2. Stop the Nightmares of Trauma (2000)
3. Tapping the Healer Within (2001)

For further information on TFT, contact:

> Thought Field Therapy
> 78-816 Via Carmel
> La Quinta, CA 92253
> Phone: 800-359-2873

(The author, James C. Schaefer, is not affiliated with TFT.)

Chapter 52 TFT – VOICE TECHNOLOGY VERSUS DIAGNOSTIC THERAPIST

TFT treatment of clinical cases is provided in two ways: Voice Technology or a diagnostic therapist. (Dr. Bray is a diagnostic therapist.) Dr. Roger J. Callahan clearly believes that Voice Technology is the more effective method. In his 2000 book, "Stop the Nightmares of Trauma," Dr. Callahan states, "Today I treat everyone with the more powerful Voice Technology over the telephone."

I used both methods, and I want to comment on their effectiveness. In the early days, prior to the December 1998 breakthrough, neither method seemed effective. However, the diagnostic method was definitely the better of the two. After the December breakthrough, both methods worked better. But the diagnostic method was better by far, with maybe a 90% success rate. Meanwhile, the success rate for Voice Technology was about 25 per cent. (These statistics are based on my general impression, not a detailed statistical analysis.)

TFT is much different than talk therapy. If you're in talk therapy, you hope you'll get some results in six months. With TFT, you'll get results in a much shorter time frame–immediate to maybe 24 hours. So TFT has one hell of an advantage over any other psychotherapy.

The drawback to TFT, and this occurred in my case, is that sometimes it doesn't have any noticeable effect at all. I've described this in an earlier chapter titled "TFT – FAILED ATTEMPTS."

Once TFT started working for me on a regular basis, I expected the results of TFT treatments to occur according to the "immediate to 24 hours" standard. I'll give an example. Assume I bought a pair of tennis shoes and encountered a phobic trigger. I would get tense and feel uncomfortable. Frequently, my eyes would bother me. I knew I would be throwing away those tennis shoes at 2:00 a.m. My solution was to seek TFT treatment that same day. I considered it imperative that I be treated before I went to bed that night.

If I saw Dr. Bray, there was a 90% chance I would keep the tennis shoes. If I used Voice Technology, there was a 25% chance of keeping the shoes. If the treatment was effective, my tension would go away within a few minutes to maybe an hour. Also, I wouldn't wake up at 2:00 a.m. In other words, TFT gave me results within the 24 hours standard. (My two breakthrough sessions were major exceptions to the 24 hours standard. For those sessions, it took about a month before results occurred.)

I'll give an illustration that suggests Voice Technology may be less effective than use of in-person TFT therapy. Sometimes when I used Voice Technology, it gave me enough help so that I didn't throw away the product at 2:00 a.m. However I wasn't feeling well when I got up the next morning, and I knew the product I'd purchased was causing my discomfort. Then I would see Dr. Bray, and his TFT treatment would fully resolve the matter. In other words, Voice Technology was only able to partially solve the problem. This type of situation occurred a number of times. (On the other hand, there were two occasions where Voice Technology solved a problem for me that Dr. Bray had not been able to resolve.)

Note that these treatments didn't resolve my basic buying problem. They only allowed me to keep the item I'd purchased, but that was no small accomplishment.

I checked with a Voice Technology therapist on its apparently relatively low success rate. I was told that I should have called back when the tapping had been unsuccessful. (I usually saw Dr. Bray instead.)

Even though Voice Technology had only a 25% success rate for me, it has a spectacular advantage. It is available 7 days a week and from 6:00 a.m. to 9:00 p.m. (I achieved this extensive coverage by using two different therapists.) Voice Technology has a second, spectacular advantage: It can be used from anywhere in the world! Just pick up the phone and call.

Voice Technology is not cheap. The rates in December 2001 were $200-$500 per hour, depending on the therapist. You only pay for the length of time you're on the phone. After you've had a little experience using Voice Technology, you can normally resolve the problem in a few minutes. My calls usually cost me $20 to $50 each.

(It's my understanding that health insurance will normally not cover the costs of Voice Technology treatments.)

I think you should use a diagnostic therapist for the initial TFT treatment, so he or she can teach the tapping techniques and show you the exact locations on the body to be tapped.

When you have a problem that will require a lengthy description and analysis, I think use of a diagnostic therapist is the preferred method. In-person communication is better than talking over a phone, and a diagnostic therapist charges less per hour.

Use of a diagnostic therapist has one other advantage. The results of arm tests provide immediate, solid feedback to the client. I felt more confident of those affirmations than the Voice Technology therapist's remark that there were, for example, "no perturbations present."

In summary, my success with Voice Technology did not match the claims made for it. However, I did have some success with it—often at times when no other help was available. My advice is that you try both the diagnostic therapist and Voice Technology. Determine for yourself what works for you. If you try only one of the methods, you haven't fully tested TFT's capabilities.

Chapter 53 CHIROPRACTIC TREATMENTS

I've seen maybe 30 different chiropractors over the last 25 years. Although their adjustments didn't always hold very long, I thought their overall performance was magnificent. First, they solved my initial, severe back problem. Then when my back problem would reoccur, they provided the help I needed to carry on my daily activities. Usually they treated me the same day I called them.

I've been in chiropractor offices hundreds of times over the years. I've never seen a patient whose condition looked as bad as mine on my first chiropractor visit.

My impression is that people are often reluctant to see a chiropractor. If you have a back problem, have seen a medical doctor, and your condition isn't improving, give the chiropractor a try.

Because I went to a chiropractor so often, I knew how my recovery should proceed after I had been adjusted. If I saw the chiropractor in the morning and wasn't feeling noticeably better late that afternoon, I'd go back to see him again that same day. He would adjust me again. I think that in those twice in a day instances, I was not properly adjusted the first time, or my back had gone out again during the day. The occasions where I saw a chiropractor twice in one day occurred maybe a dozen times over a 25-year period.

For patients with a back problem, the emphasis is usually on the lower back. However, the chiropractor will also usually adjust the upper back, by applying a quick downward pressure. Keep your mouth slightly open during this procedure, to allow the air from your lungs to be expelled.

All the chiropractors I saw used basically the same techniques. However, the results varied. Only about 1 in 5 chiropractors could successfully adjust me—certainly not a flattering statistic for the chiropractic profession. In other words, my back would be out again within 24 hours after I was adjusted. Quite a few chiropractors commented that I wasn't easy to adjust. So my suggestion is that if you don't get good results with the first chiropractor you see, try at least two more.

Very few chiropractors do "muscle testing." If your adjustments don't hold very long (i.e., your back is out again in a couple days), try to see a chiropractor who does muscle testing. The muscle testing may show that you need further treatment using the "activator." However, I want to note that it appears very few patients require muscle testing or activator treatment. (The extended arm testing done in TFT is "muscle testing.")

I once read a summary of a study that was done to measure the effectiveness of chiropractors as compared to medical doctors in treating back problems. The study indicated chiropractors were somewhat more effective. Although the study favored chiropractors, I didn't think much of the study because it ignored cases like mine. In my case, the medical doctors had no treatment at all, while the chiropractor was able to resolve the problem.

In December 2001, my chiropractor in San Diego was charging $40 for an office visit, with a 10% discount for prompt payment—i.e., $36 if you paid the day of the visit.

When my back went out, my hips always shifted to the right. One chiropractor told me the nontechnical term for my condition was "sidewinder."

The medical chart for a few of my chiropractic treatments is shown in Appendix A.

Chapter 54 NORGESIC PILLS

As I indicated in earlier chapters, I used Norgesic tablets for my sciatic pain. I found the tablets gave me 100% pain relief. I once tried a different brand of muscle relaxant, and it wasn't nearly as effective.

Norgesic prescriptions come with a "may cause drowsiness" warning. Even when I took 8 tablets a day, I didn't experience any drowsiness. The tablets contain quite a bit of aspirin. A more likely side effect is a slightly upset stomach. However, I never found that to be a significant problem.

I tried using Norgesic tablets to reduce the frequency of my "back out" problem, but I didn't find that the tablets produced any noticeable effect.

Apparently, the tablets are no longer a popular prescription drug. The Kaiser Permanente HMO hasn't included Norgesic tablets in its formulary for quite a few years–i.e., to get Norgesic tablets you have to ask for them and pay for them.

Based on my experience, I recommend Norgesic tablets for relief of sciatic pain.

Chapter 55 REPORT THE RECOVERY PERCENTAGE

Psychotherapy has been in use for over 100 years without being clearly validated by experience or a scientific study. At the rate we're going, the effectiveness of psychotherapy won't be determined in the next 100 years either.

I think this problem can be solved by making more information available to the public and to medical administrators. The key is to provide information on the results of treatment–i.e., did the patient recover?

Two items of information are needed: (1) per cent that the patient has recovered, and (2) the type of psychotherapy being practiced (psychoanalysis, TFT, etc.). For patients covered by health insurance, the claim form would be the vehicle to provide this information.

The per cent that the patient has recovered would be supplied by the therapist. Presumably, this will result in the therapist and patient discussing the degree of recovery that has occurred. After all, the therapist has only "some idea" of the recovery percentage. He or she will require input from the patient to determine the figure to be reported.

When the therapist is submitting claims directly to the insurance company, he or she would be required to give the patient a copy of the claim form whenever the recovery percentage is increased. In other words, the patient would always be informed as to the recovery per cent that is reported.

The type of psychotherapy being practiced could be supplied in the "modifier" column on the claim form. The therapist currently enters a "procedure number" to the form. The "modifier" is the standard way of providing additional information about the procedure.

The claim form already provides all the data required for statistical analysis: diagnosis, date of illness, date of illness onset if a reoccurrence, dates of treatment, date of birth, etc.

Since HMOs do not use a claim form, they could design their own form to capture the same information. They also would be required to furnish the patient with a copy of the form whenever the recovery percentage is increased.

The new data would then be used for statistical analyses of psychotherapy treatments. The analyses should show the average per cent of recovery, average number of treatments (sessions), and number of patients that were treated. The data should be shown by diagnosis and type of psychotherapy. The statistical reports would be by calendar year. A sample report is shown below. (Reports in a real-life environment would need to provide for a much larger number of diagnoses and psychotherapies.)

CALENDAR YEAR 2002

**** HYPNOTHERAPY ****

Diagnosis	Average Age	Patients	Sessions (Average)	Average % Recovered
Anxiety	30	200	15	10%
Depression	26	150	10	20%
Phobia	40	100	23	15%
TOTAL	31	450	15	14%

Patients with more than one disorder would be classified under the diagnosis that is the most severe.

The reports would give an indication of the general level of effectiveness of psychotherapy. Obviously, such reports would make it easy to compare one type of psychotherapy against another. Also, these recovery statistics would make it easy to identify the one-third of patients who do not recover in two years, and they are the ones that should be receiving special attention.

HMOs and insurance companies would be required to make the analyses available to the general public.

I was given six sessions of psychotherapy at Kaiser Permanente in 1990, and I recovered zero per cent. As best I can recall, the psychologist and I never discussed my lack of improvement. I think it's safe to say the psychologist (and Kaiser management) didn't receive proper feedback. How could they monitor and improve their operations without feedback?

I think this lack of feedback is common in the psychotherapy industry. It applies to big operations like Kaiser, and also to the many psychologists who work in small, one to six-person offices. In my own case, there were several times when I saw a psychologist for a period of time, got irritated with the progress, and finally phoned and canceled the next session. And that would be the end of contact. In other words, even the psychologist often doesn't know how his or her patient fared–because there is nothing in the psychotherapy process that forces a discussion regarding the per cent of recovery that has occurred.

I think the gathering of information on the per cent of recovery would primarily benefit the public; however, the feedback would also be valuable to therapists. They would be able to tell more precisely how effective their treatments are.

If a doctor prescribes medicine to control high blood pressure, we expect him or her to record the blood pressure readings after the medicine has been taken for a certain period of time. Similarly, I think psychologists should record the recovery per cent after a period of psychotherapy.

Medical treatments always involve issues of confidentiality. The diagnosis (e.g., depression, phobia, etc.) is a sensitive piece of information, and it is presently being recorded. I think the two new items of data (recovery per cent and type of psychotherapy) should be processed according to confidentiality guidelines presently used for the diagnosis.

In an earlier chapter, I referred to an article on psychotherapy in the November 1995 issue of Consumer Reports. The article presented statistics on the effectiveness of psychotherapy. That article contains the following statements:

> Our survey . . . is a unique look at what happens in real life, where problems are diverse and less well-defined, and where some therapists try one technique after another until something works. The success of

therapy under these real-life conditions has never before been well studied, says Martin Seligman, former director of clinical training in psychology at the University of Pennsylvania and past president of the American Psychological Association's division of clinical psychology.

What a bombshell. Here is an authoritative person saying that the recovery rate statistics used for psychotherapy are generally not based on patients treated under real-life conditions. In other words, statistics on the effectiveness of psychotherapy are usually obtained from research projects. Obviously, what is needed are statistics for patients treated in regular clinical settings.

I was the systems analyst in charge of the San Diego County jail computer system for ten years. We had nine computer-prepared statistical reports that provided information on the number of inmates incarcerated, type of crimes committed, number of days the inmates were in jail, etc. I can assure you those reports were based on real inmates in real jails.

I think it's generally known that drugs can only be prescribed after they have passed research studies and have been approved by the FDA (Food and Drug Administration). Even after the requirements have been met, drugs often fail when they are prescribed for the general population. Those drugs must be withdrawn from the market. In short, what works in a test situation may not work in a real-life environment.

Psychotherapy shouldn't get any special handling. Psychologists should be required to provide information based on results with patients in regular (not research) clinical settings–along the lines that I've suggested here.

I recognize that research psychologists would object to using these recovery percentages because they are "subjective." Yet subjective assessments can be quite useful. In the computer field, a manager will normally assign his or her "best" systems analysts to the most difficult projects. That method works quite well, even though the determination of "best" is subjective.

The consumers of psychological services in today's environment have very little on which to evaluate different therapies. Any ratings–even subjective ones–would be most welcome.

If objective ratings were desired, that could certainly be accomplished. Simply design a form with questions appropriate for each type of neurosis. For depression, ask the person to report how frequently he or she cries. For compulsive disorders, ask the person to report how much time is spent each day on unwanted repetitive behavior. I'm just trying to present the general idea here. Presumably there would be multiple questions for each type of neurosis.

Some time later, say 2 to 6 months, the patient would be asked to complete the form again. If the person reported that he or she was no longer crying and no longer spending time on compulsive acts, a recovery percentage of 100% would be appropriate. (Psychologists already have "rating scales" similar to what I'm suggesting. However, their use appears to be limited, and I doubt one could easily ascertain a recovery percentage by looking at the "rating scale.")

Ideally, there should be a scientific study comparing each major type of psychotherapy against a control group. Although that would be desirable, the psychology books I've read have consistently pointed out how difficult it is to devise such a study. In short, it appears that type of study is seldom done. To my knowledge, no landmark study of that type has ever been done.

In line with the above comments, the 1995 textbook, "Abnormal Psychology," (D. L. Rosenhan and M. E. Seligman) contains the following statements with regard to psychotherapies:

> Claims for success are broad but the evidence is slim. Only a few controlled tests have been conducted to assess the effectiveness of particular therapies, and even fewer tests have been done to compare the relative efficacy of various treatments.

It seems like reporting the additional data (recovery per cent and type of therapy) will have to suffice. If the data is reported and the appropriate statistical reports are produced, I predict the following will occur:

1. Administrators will become aware that very few clients are recovering in the maximum number of outpatient sessions (annually) that are now commonly covered by insurance policies. (At Kaiser

Permanente, my coverage currently provides for a maximum of 20 sessions per year. For certain diagnoses, there is no 20-session limit.)

2. Administrators will find recovery percentages are abysmally low. For many patients, the recovery per cent will be zero.

3. Administrators will recognize certain therapies are more effective than others. (All talk therapies will produce about the same recovery rates. But administrators will now have statistics on non-talk therapies–e.g., TFT, hypnotherapy, desensitization exercises by behaviorists, etc.) I think non-talk therapies will show much higher recovery rates–i.e., non-talk therapies will push talk therapies off the map.

4. Administrators will act on the new information that is available– because they usually are not psychologists themselves. That is, the matter will be out of the psychologists' control. My highest hope is with the administrators. They are motivated by budget considerations and are not committed to a particular psychotherapy.

5. Administrators will require treatments based on the type of neurosis. For example, patients with depression might see psychiatrists, while those with phobias would see behaviorists. Now we pretty much use a given type of psychotherapy for any neurosis. A psychiatrist will tend to use psychoanalysis-based therapy, regardless of which neurosis you have–i.e., one technique for all neuroses.

I recognize that most psychotherapists claim their orientation is "eclectic." However, each of the therapists I saw never deviated from his or her basic approach–i.e., the TFT therapist used TFT techniques, the hypnotherapist used hypnosis, etc.

6. Administrators will begin dropping certain kinds of psychotherapists from the payroll. (This relates to item 3 above.)

7. Administrators will begin concentrating on the one-third of patients that don't improve at all. With better statistics, it will be easier to compare patients who improve with those who do not.

8.   Administrators will appreciate the recovery percentage as a built-in practice for evaluating new types of psychotherapy.

9.   Administrators will use the statistics to bring about more extensive mental health insurance coverage. It is possible that the statistics will show the therapies have only marginal value–i.e., the recovery rates are only slightly higher than the 67% recovery rate that apparently occurs for people who do not receive treatment. Then it will be hard to get broadened insurance coverage.

One other possibility is that the statistics may show that the recovery rate for a given neurosis is 90% or higher. If it could be shown, for example, that phobias can be treated with a 90% success rate, health insurance regulations could be changed to cover phobia treatments.

10. Administrators will bring about better results for patients with neuroses, via the activities listed in the above items.

I doubt there will be any great rush to gather statistics as I described here. So I would like to suggest that the appropriate authorities designate three separate sites to accumulate these new statistics. Presumably the three sites would be providers of extensive psychotherapy services and located in different regions of the United States.

HMOs and insurance companies could implement the statistics-gathering concept at any time–i.e., they don't need to wait for the 3-site idea to be implemented. Basically, this is a minor change in administrative procedures, yet it could lead to better treatment of patients and significantly improved management of mental health resources.

Chapter 56 SUMMARY

For the individual with a neurosis, or suffering from a physical problem with a psychological basis, I've given some suggestions that may help to resolve the problem. To summarize, I suggested:

1. Check your current environment for conditions that might be causing your psychological illness.
2. Use the 3-week vacation technique to expose psychological illnesses.
3. Try to find words and pictures that your mind has misinterpreted.
4. Use Thought Field Therapy (TFT) if you need "professional help" for a psychological problem.

For the field of psychology, I presented three issues.

1. The key to my case was a misinterpreted word. Psychologists need to develop techniques to find misinterpreted words (and pictures) that are causing a neurosis—not an easy task.
2. A manual should be prepared to help patients, psychologists and primary care physicians in determining the appropriate psychotherapy for a given neurosis. The manual should contain a chart for each neurosis. Each chart should show:
   a. Name of the neurosis
   b. Type of psychotherapy most effective for the neurosis
   c. Number of treatments normally required
   d. Recovery rate
   e. Relapse rate

    f. Recommended prescription drugs, plus remarks on side effects.

I should note that such a manual would not be easy to prepare, because very few statistics are currently being captured on several of the above items.

3. Millions of Americans suffer from illnesses that are classified as neuroses, and it costs billions of dollars to treat them—usually through psychotherapy. Yet we don't know to what degree the psychotherapy is effective, or the illnesses which it helps. We could answer those questions if we simply had psychotherapists report two pieces of information (per cent that the patient has recovered and type of psychotherapy), and then presented that data in statistical reports.

If HMOs and insurance companies would implement these statistical practices, patient treatment would improve, and the savings would be astronomical.

I described my neurosis as a phobia, because that was the most severe aspect of my illness. However, I also had aspects of obsessive-compulsive disorder and anxiety.

I think this book is unique in that it identified in detail the key steps that occurred in the recovery process for a case that involved a neurosis and physical problems with a psychological basis. Hopefully, it will be a model that will help others to recovery.

HOW TO CONTACT THE AUTHOR

The author can be contacted at the following address:

JAMES C. SCHAEFER
P. O. BOX 600039
SAN DIEGO, CA. 92160-0039

If you would like a reply, please enclose a stamped, self-addressed envelope.

No e-mail messages, please.

NOTE: It's possible that over the years the P. O. box number may change. It is my intention to always have my current box number on this page.

APPENDIX "A" – CHIROPRACTOR CHART

PATIENT: Schaefer, James C.

DATE	TIME	TREATMENT AND FINDINGS
Jan 02 1988	1:11P	(K) Std. Exam, PI on rt 1½", lt 1/4", L.5 lt, D.6, D.3, ASR TOG (en)
Jan 13 1988	7:05P	(M) PI rt 2", L.5 lt, D.10 post, D.6, C.2 lt, ASR TOG, lateral femur on rt, std. exam. (mm)
Jan 27 1988	7:07P	(M) PI rt 1", L.5 lt, D.10, D.6, C.2 lt, ASR TOG. (mm)
Feb 12 1988	8:56A	(K) PI on rt less 1/4", D.12, D.6, D.3, ASR TOG, TMJ on rt closed (en)
Feb 23 1988	7:09P	(C) Rt PI 1/4", D.12, D.3, ASR TOG, no TMJ, Lumbar spine ok, patient complaints of rt hipping?, happier (en)
Feb 25 1988	7:06P	(C) Complains leg pain on rt, adj. imbrication of L.5, D.12, D.6, D.1, neck ok, TMJ ok. (mm)
Mar 02 1988	8:27A	(M) PI rt 1", L.5 lt, D.10, D.6, C.5 lt, ASR TOG. (DG)
Mar 10 1988	7:04P	(CH) rt Hip out, L.5 ok, C.1 TOG. (mm)
Mar 15 1988	7:12P	(M) L.5 lt, l.4-L.5 disc on rt, D.10, D.6, C.3 lt, ASR TOG, flattening? antalgic (en)

173

James C. Schaefer

Mar 17 1988   7:12P   (CH) Has rt hip out,
                                           acetyl joint, adj. L.5,
                                           rt acetyl joint post,
                                           D.10, D.6, D.1, C.3
                                           ASR TOG. (mm)

NOTE: This is not a copy. Information shown here was retyped from the original.